Nostalgic

LONDON

ELLIE WALKER-ARNOTT

INTRODUCTION

This book invites you to journey back in time, to immerse yourself in London's incredible 2000-year-old history, which is evident everywhere once you start looking for it. Nostalgia is a sentimentality for the past or a desire to return to a different time, perhaps a time in living memory. It might not be in yours, but everything in this book is in the city's living memory. The chapters are made up of both physical structures – the 17th-century shops, the incredible palaces, the buildings that have been added to and destroyed and then grown again from the rubble – and the stories that modern-day London is built on, and wouldn't exist without.

The addresses in this book have either been picked because they are incredibly old and still proudly standing (despite what the years have thrown at them), because they feature perfectly preserved Tudor brickwork, Victorian tiling or 1930s bathroom taps, or because they evoke a strong sense of a previous era. Sometimes a little imagination is required to conjure up a place's past while, in other cases, simply stepping through a doorway or into a room will feel like time travel.

There are countless places and buildings of historical significance that aren't in this book (you could write entire tomes on each of these chapters' subjects and still not cover everything) but it aims to be a useful and inspiring mix of iconic and surprising places. The majority are here because they are relatively easy to access, open to the public and fun to explore. They might be places you've heard of, but didn't know the stories behind, or somewhere half-forgotten – everything from a romantic cemetery and a crumbling dance hall to the oldest hat shop in the world and an abandoned train line that has been taken over with greenery.

HOW TO USE THIS BOOK

———————

This book lists over 350 things you need to know if you're visiting London and are especially interested to learn more about the city's rich and vibrant history. Most of these are places to visit, with practical information to help you find your way. Others are bits of information that help you get to know the city and its past. The aim of this guide is to inspire and to help you see London through different eyes, not to cover the city from A to Z.

The places listed in this guide are given an address, including the area, and a number. The area and number allow you to find the locations on the maps at the beginning of the book: first look for the corresponding map (for example Map 1 of Soho, Covent Garden and Holborn or Map 4 of Kensington and Chelsea), then look for the right number. A word of caution however: these maps are not detailed enough to allow you to find specific locations in the city. You can obtain an excellent map from any tourist office or in most hotels, and of course you can locate the addresses on your smartphone.

Please bear in mind that this book obviously focusses on just one of the many sides of London, and that the selection of addresses presented is highly personal. You might not always agree with it, or you might find a certain place is missing. If you want to leave a comment, recommend a spot or reveal your favourite nostalgic place, please follow @500hiddensecrets on Instagram or Facebook and get in touch with the publisher. And of course it's always a good idea to visit our website *www.the500hiddensecrets.com,* where you'll find lots of new content, freshly updated info and travel inspiration about London and many other destinations.

ABOUT THE AUTHOR

ELLIE WALKER-ARNOTT lives in North London with her partner Tom and their cat Ginger. She works as a writer and editor, currently at *Time Out London* where she's Digital Editor and editor of the magazine's UK Escapes section. It's a job that has introduced her to countless cool and lesser-known corners of the city and allows her to champion her home city every day.

A fan of London's wild green spaces, buzzy urban villages and unlikely pockets of calm, Ellie's been in love with London for as long as she can remember. Writing this book, as well as snooping around inside ancient buildings and wandering down atmospheric alleyways in search of places to feature, has been a total joy. She felt sure she knew a lot of London's past before beginning this project, but now she can feel layers upon layers of history wherever she walks.

Ellie would like to thank all the generous people – friends, colleagues and strangers – who offered up their recommendations and shared their knowledge of London's timeless, historic spots. Emma, Emily, Hannah, Ellie and Tori deserve a special mention for patiently listening to hours of book chat over the past year. Thanks to Dettie and Marc at Luster and to Sam for bringing the book to life with his photographs. Thanks also to Mum for always being there to lend a hand, to Liz for kindly volunteering to be a second pair of eyes and to Tom for being an eager exploring companion (especially when it came to nostalgic pub crawls) and not complaining when it seemed like Ellie spent more time writing in Hornsey Library than she did at home.

LONDON

overview

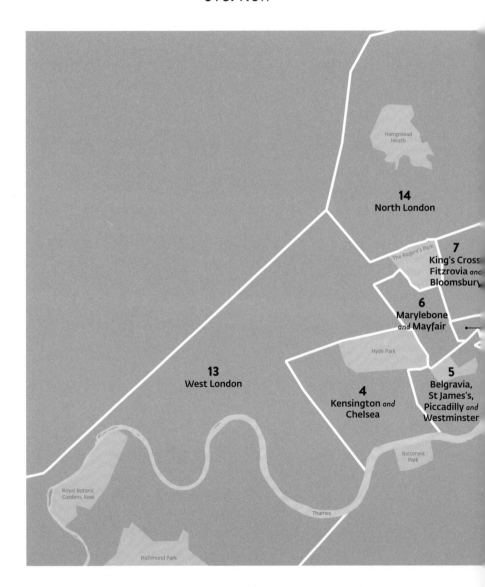

Hampstead
Heath

14
North London

The Regent's Park

7
King's Cross
Fitzrovia *and*
Bloomsbury

6
Marylebone
and **Mayfair**

Hyde Park

13
West London

4
Kensington *and*
Chelsea

5
Belgravia,
St James's,
Piccadilly *and*
Westminster

Battersea
Park

Royal Botanic
Gardens, Kew

Thames

Richmond Park

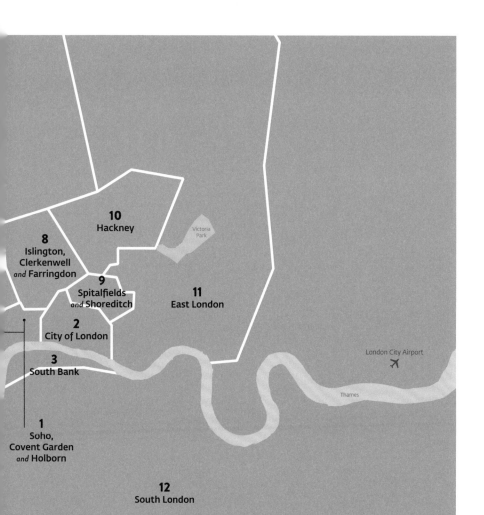

10
Hackney

8
Islington,
Clerkenwell
and Farringdon

9
Spitalfields
and Shoreditch

Victoria
Park

11
East London

2
City of London

London City Airport

3
South Bank

Thames

1
Soho,
Covent Garden
and Holborn

12
South London

Map 1
SOHO, COVENT GARDEN
and HOLBORN

Red Lion
Square
Gardens

Drake St.

Gray's Inn Rd

Hatton Garden

97

54

292

Farringdon St.

348

High Holborn

326

150

311

173

Holborn

Lincoln's Inn
Fields

Chancery Ln

Fetter Ln

Farringdon St.

Kingsway

295

Fleet St

294

315

206

Royal
Opera
House

180

149

Strand

Middle
Temple
Gardens

Inner
Temple
Gardens

188

269

266

84

297

Somerset
House

185

277

148

Victoria Embankment

336

Blackfriars Bridge

Waterloo Bridge

Thames

Victoria
Embankment
Gardens

Bernie
Spain
Gardens

Map 2
CITY OF LONDON

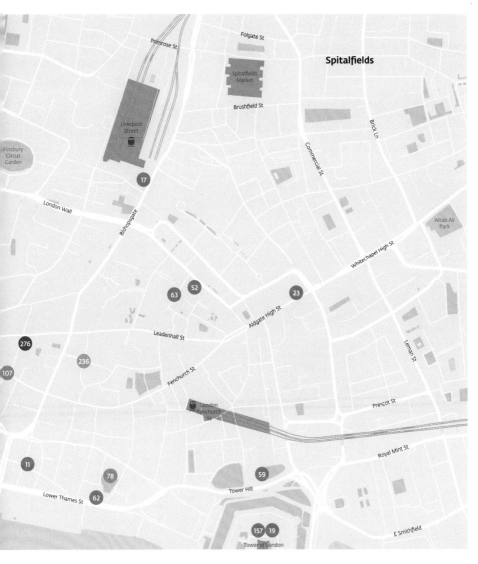

Spitalfields

Folgate St

Primrose St

Spitalfields Market

Brushfield St

Brick Ln

Liverpool Street

Finsbury Circus Garden

(17)

London Wall

Bishopsgate

Altab Ali Park

Commercial St

Whitechapel High St

(63) (52)

(23)

Aldgate High St

Leadenhall St

Leman St

(276)

(236)

Fenchurch St

(107)

London Fenchurch St

Prescot St

Royal Mint St

(11)

(78)

(59)

Lower Thames St

(62)

Tower Hill

E Smithfield

(157) (19)

Tower of London

Map 3
SOUTH BANK

City of London

Cannon Street

London Fenchurch Street

Lower Thames St

Southwark Bridge

London Bridge

Tower of London

Thames

Southwark Bridge Road

81 42

41

90

193

Tower Bridge

293

Tooley St

Potters Fields Park

London Bridge

2

Borough High St

Tooley St

104

Leathermarket Gardens

Bermondsey St

Tanner St Park

Jamaica Rd

Long Ln

Tower Bridge Rd

Great Dover St

Tabard Gardens

Map 4
KENSINGTON and CHELSEA

Bayswater Rd

Notting Hill Gt

Holland Park Ave

100

327

147
Kensington Palace

Round Pond

Hyde Park

The Serpentine

Holland Park

119

136

Kensington High St

Kensington Rd

Royal Albert Hall **67**

179

Earls Ct Rd

Kensington

102

Queen's Gate

161
Natural History Museum

255 **160**
V&A Museum

Brompton Rd

Warwick Rd

Cromwell Rd

34

W Cromwell Rd

Earls Ct Rd

283

Old Brompton Rd

Warwick Rd

Chelsea

199

Redcliffe Gardens

Fulham Rd

238

King's Rd

Finborough Rd

46

86

139

108

38

DISCOVERIES — PLACES — BUILDINGS — ART & CULTURE — SHOPS — FOOD — DRINK — STAYS

Map 5
BELGRAVIA, ST JAMES'S, PICCADILLY *and* WESTMINSTER

Map 6
MARYLEBONE *and* MAYFAIR

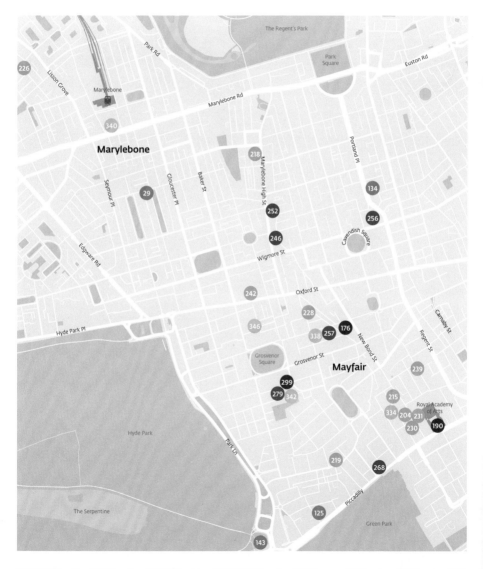

The Regent's Park

Park Rd

226

Lisson Grove

Marylebone

Park Square

Euston Rd

340

Marylebone Rd

Marylebone

Portland Pl

218

Seymour Pl

Gloucester Pl

Baker St

Marylebone High St

29

134

252

256

Cavendish Square

246

Wigmore St

242

Oxford St

Carnaby St

228

346

New Bond St

Regent St

338 257 176

Grosvenor Square

Grosvenor St

Mayfair

239

Hyde Park Pl

Edgware Rd

299

215

279 342

334

Royal Academy
of Arts

204 231

230

190

Hyde Park

Park Ln

219

268

The Serpentine

125

Green Park

143

DISCOVERIES — PLACES — BUILDINGS — **ART & CULTURE** — SHOPS — **FOOD** — **DRINK** — STAYS

Map 7
KING'S CROSS, FITZROVIA
and BLOOMSBURY

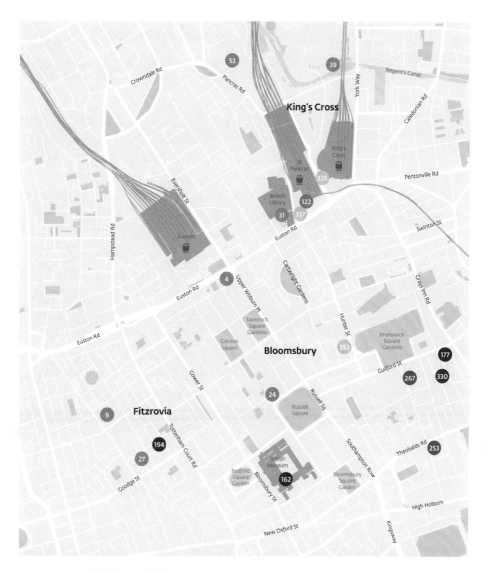

DISCOVERIES — PLACES — BUILDINGS — ART & CULTURE — SHOPS — FOOD — DRINK — STAYS

Map 8
ISLINGTON, CLERKENWELL
and FARRINGDON

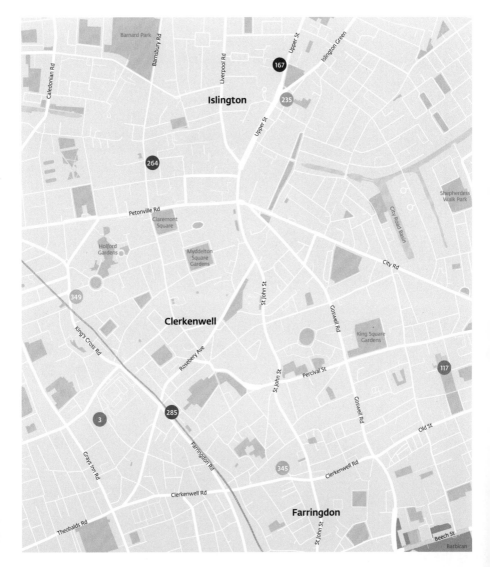

Map 9
SPITALFIELDS
and SHOREDITCH

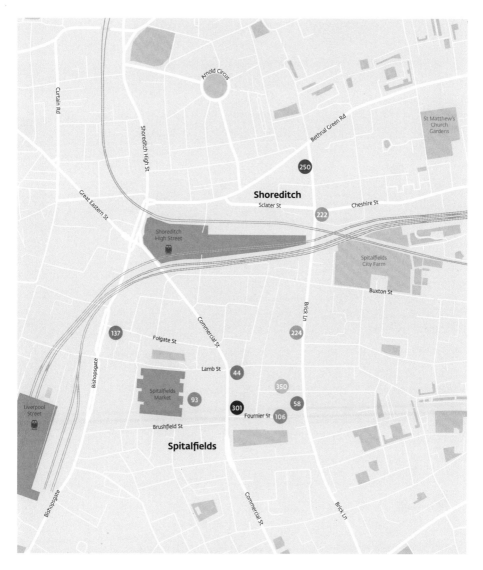

Map 10
HACKNEY

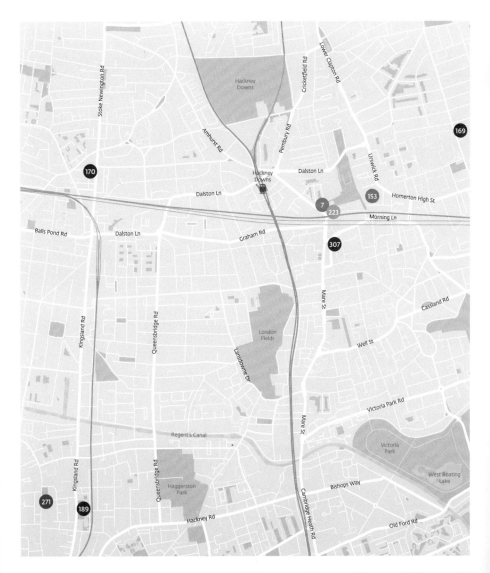

Map 11
EAST LONDON

Map 12

SOUTH LONDON

London City Airport

290

Southwark Park

Lower Rd

Evelyn Street

Old Kent Rd

83

47

Thames

Woolwich Rd

82

Romney Rd

40 25

77

144

Greenwich Park

Shooters Hill Rd

Shooters Hill Rd
Blackheath

Academy Rd

Well Hall Rd

6

Peckham Rye Park & Common

329

164

Forest Hill Rd

Brownhill Rd

135

Sidcup Rd

196

Southend Ln

ystal Palace Park

79

Beckenham Place Park

Map 13
WEST LONDON

Map 14
NORTH LONDON

DISCOVERIES

UNDERGROUND

secrets

---

1 **CRYSTAL PALACE SUBWAY**

Crystal Palace Parade
SE19 1XX
South ⑬
cpsubway.org.uk

Built as an entrance to the grand Crystal Palace, this ornate Victorian subway is a real subterranean stunner. The abandoned space is made up of an elegantly vaulted ceiling and pillars built out of orange and white bricks. Since the Crystal Palace burned down in the 1930s and the railway line closed, it's not seen much action but it's opened to the public a handful of times a year, while the Friends of Crystal Palace Subway work to preserve it for the local community.

2 **BASCULE CHAMBER**

AT: TOWER BRIDGE
Tower Bridge Road
SE1 2UP
South Bank ②
+44 (0)20 7403 3761
towerbridge.org.uk/ basculechamber

Possibly the most famous landmark in London, Tower Bridge is an iconic structure that has been straddling the River Thames since the 1880s. It's an impressive sight, with its grand turreted towers and modern glass walkway, but it's hiding something equally remarkable underground: the Bascule Chamber, a huge, subterranean space constructed to allow the movement of the bridge's counterweights when the bridge lifts up. Understandably, it's not always open to the public, but it's sometimes used as a stunning venue for concerts and art installations.

3 MAIL RAIL

AT: THE POSTAL MUSEUM
15-20 Phoenix Place
WC1X 0DA
Clerkenwell ⑧
+44 (0)30 0030 0700
postalmuseum.org

London has a second, secret underground system deep under the city. It's like the Tube, but for the city's mail instead. Built by the Post Office more than a century ago, the train network moved packages, postcards and parcels across the city through six-and-a-half miles (10,5 kilometres) of underground tunnel. It was taken out of service in 2003, but a stretch of the tunnel has recently been reopened as part of the Postal Museum. Visitors can now make like a letter and ride the rails on a tiny Tube train.

4 THE CRYPT GALLERY

165 Euston Road
NW1 2BA
Bloomsbury ⑦
+44 (0)20 7388 1461
cryptgallery.org

Beneath an imposing church on busy Euston Road there's an art gallery with a difference. Once a crypt used for coffin burials in the 1800s, the cavern beneath the church is now an atmospheric exhibition and creative events space. Head underground (access is through a red door on the side of the church) to find the spot, which is still the final resting place of 557 Londoners.

5 CHURCHILL WAR ROOMS

King Charles St
SW1A 2AQ
Westminster ⑤
+44 (0)20 7416 5000
iwm.org.uk/churchill-war-rooms

Under the streets of Westminster, there's a network of secret bunkers that were used by Prime Minister Winston Churchill during WWII. The rooms acted as a command centre for the government as, above ground, London was being bombed during the Blitz. It's now an underground museum where you can wander through the offices, meeting rooms and living quarters that have been preserved exactly as they were when they were abandoned at the end of the war in 1945. It's a fascinating and atmospheric place where you can really feel the history around you.

1 CRYSTAL PALACE SUBWAY

Timeless
TOWERS

---

6 SEVERNDROOG CASTLE

Castle Wood
SE18 3RT
South ⑫
+44 (0)80 0689 1796
*severndroog
castle.org.uk*

For exceptional views of the sprawling city, head to Severndroog Castle. The 18th-century Gothic folly tops Shooters Hill, one of London's highest points. The tower didn't have practical aspirations, but since being built in 1784, it's been used as a surveying point for a detailed map of England and was manned 24 hours a day as an air raid defence during the Blitz. Take it all in from the 360-degree viewing platform before visiting the castle's tearoom.

7 ST AUGUSTINE'S TOWER

Mare St
(adjacent to nr 354)
E8 1HT
Hackney ⑩
+44 (0)20 8986 0029
staugustinestower.org

The oldest building in Hackney, this church tower stands solo after the rest of the structure was demolished in 1798. These days you can climb up the ancient spiral staircase to the top to peer out over East London's ever-changing landscape. Just think, it was built during the 13th century, when Hackney was a rural village outside of London's city borders, but now the tower finds itself in a fully urban environment.

8 ST MARY'S TOWER HORNSEY

High St
N8 7NT
North ⑭
*hornseychurch
tower.com*

It doesn't look much like one these days, but Hornsey is the oldest recorded village in London, and this medieval tower is one of its last, original remnants. Surrounded by Victorian pubs and new-build flats, it's all that remains of the 15th-century parish church that once stood on this spot. The space where the rest of the church used to be is now a garden tended by volunteers. Popular with dog walkers and gardenless locals, it's a peaceful and special place to pause.

8 ST MARY'S TOWER HORNSEY

9 BT TOWER

60 Cleveland St
W1T 4JZ
Fitzrovia ⑦

From 1964 until the 1980s, this cylindrical London landmark was the tallest building in the city. It was built by the General Post Office to support microwave aerials that carried telecommunications transmissions out of London to the rest of the country – and was topped by a flashy revolving restaurant. The modernist tower is still used for communications, but the building is no longer open to the general public (except during the annual Open House festival). Get a good view by looking skywards almost anywhere in Fitzrovia.

10 CALEDONIAN PARK CLOCK TOWER

Market Road
N7 9PL
North ⑭
islington.gov.uk

An elegant, white tower in Cally Park is one of London's newest viewpoints, but the building itself is anything but. Built in 1855, the restored clock tower was once the centrepiece of Caledonian Market, an enormous shopping area where you could buy anything from a bull to a china teacup. With the market now closed, the tower offers visitors a sweet vantage point from which to see the city.

11 THE MONUMENT

Fish St Hill
EC3R 8AH
City of London ②
+44 (0)20 7403 3761
themonument.org.uk

It might not seem very tall by today's standards but The Monument is a mighty memorial. Constructed in the 1670s, it stands to commemorate the Great Fire of London and the rebuilding of the city, which had largely been destroyed by the flames. It's located a loaf's throw from Pudding Lane, where the fire began in a baker's house in 1666. Climb the 311 steps to the viewing platform for a new perspective on the city and its history.

Icons of
INDUSTRY

12 **BATTERSEA POWER STATION**

188 Kirtling St
SW8 5BP
South ⑫
+44 (0)20 7501 0688
*battersea
powerstation.co.uk*

A great hulk of a building, Battersea's enormous power station is an instantly recognisable London landmark. Built in the 1930s, it's one of the biggest brick buildings on the planet, but it's more famous for appearing on Pink Floyd's *Animals* album cover, complete with a huge, floating, inflatable pink pig. It was decommissioned in the 1970s and then remained empty for decades, with talk of it being turned into countless things, from a theme park to a football stadium. It's now being redeveloped into housing, with restaurants and bars spilling out onto the riverside, but the shape of the original construction, which is Grade II-listed, remains intact.

13 **TATE MODERN**

Bankside
SE1 9TG
South Bank ③
+44 (0)20 7887 8888
tate.org.uk/modern

Set on the south side of the Thames, Bankside Power Station once generated electricity for the city. The stunning structure you can see today was built in two phases, between 1947 and 1963, with an enormous turbine hall and a single chimney. It closed in the early 1980s and is now the site of the Tate Modern art gallery. The redevelopment preserved and made great use of the original features and you can still get a vivid sense of them today. The Turbine Hall is now a cavernous entrance and installation space, while you can find exhibitions running in the former boiler house and large concrete tanks.

14 ALEXANDRA PALACE

Alexandra Palace
Way
N22 7AY
North ⑭
+44 (0)20 8365 2121
alexandrapalace.com

A Victorian beauty on top of a hill in North London, Alexandra Palace is always a hive of activity, with gigs, conventions, an indoor ice rink, a boating lake and plenty more things to do. Known as the 'People's Palace', it's been a space for public entertainment since the 1870s. Though you wouldn't necessarily notice during a visit, Ally Pally, as it is affectionately known, is also the birthplace of television. In 1935, the BBC leased the eastern part of the building and, with the help of a huge mast that you can still see today, made the first ever public television transmissions in 1936.

15 THE HOUSE MILL

Three Mill Lane
E3 3DU
East ⑪
+44 (0)20 8980 4626
housemill.org.uk

A relic of the early industrial revolution, the House Mill in East London is the largest surviving tidal mill in the world. The current construction was built in 1776, but 1086's Domesday Book records mills on the exact same spot. The House Mill was used to produce flour for London's bakers, as well as gin during the 18th century. The huge wheels no longer turn, but the fascinating, Grade I-listed building is open regularly for tours.

16 CROSSNESS PUMPING STATION

Bazalgette Way
Abbey Wood
SE2 9AQ
+44 (0)20 8311 3711
crossness.org.uk

Trust the Victorians to make even a sewage pumping station look beautiful. This stunning waste treatment works, constructed between 1859 and 1865, features astounding colourful and ornate ironwork. It was built to improve the city's sewers, which historically emptied directly on to the shores of the Thames, and prevent further outbreaks of diseases like cholera. When the station was decommissioned in the 1950s, the building was left to rust, but much of the interior decor and machinery has now been restored, with more preservation works ongoing. The station is opened up for visitors on a number of dates each year.

HIDDEN

surprises

---

17 A PERFECTLY PRESERVED MASONIC TEMPLE

40 Liverpool St
EC2M 7QN
City of London ②
+44 (0)20 7961 1234
hyatt.com

A former Victorian railway hotel, the Andaz London Liverpool Street has been refurbished in recent years, and the builders got quite the shock. During construction, a wall was demolished and an opulent Masonic Temple, which dates back to the early 1900s, was miraculously discovered. The surprise marble and mahogany marvel, complete with a celestial ceiling and original Masons' chairs, is now one of London's not-so-well-kept secrets.

18 AN ALMOST-FORGOTTEN THEATRE

Alexandra Palace Way
N22 7AY
North ⑭
+44 (0)20 8365 2121
*theatre.
alexandrapalace.com*

The theatre inside Alexandra Palace opened in 1875 before falling into disrepair and being almost entirely forgotten about. After sitting empty for almost 80 years, the theatre was brought back to life in 2018 but the decades of neglect have become a feature of the space. Grand original plaster, paintwork and Victorian detailing have all been conserved along with any damage they've incurred over the last century, giving the theatre a romantic sense of being frozen in time.

19 THE PUB NO ONE KNOWS ABOUT

AT: TOWER OF LONDON
EC3N 4AB
City of London ②

The Tower of London is world-famous for a bunch of things: myths, legends, the Crown Jewels, Traitor's Gate, the ravens that call the castle home. But the World Heritage Site is still keeping some secrets, like the fact that there is a pub inside its ancient walls. The Keys is a tiny drinking establishment that only serves the Beefeaters, or Yeoman Warders as they are also known, that work and live at the Tower. The only way to get an invite? Make friends with a Beefeater.

AVDI · VIDE · TACE

17 A PERFECTLY PRESERVED MASONIC TEMPLE

Unusual
STREET FURNITURE

---

20 ORIGINAL GAS LAMPS

Birdcage Walk
SW1A 2BJ
Westminster ⑤

London might be one of the modern metropolises of the world, but did you know there are still around 1500 street lamps in the city that are powered by gas instead of electricity? Many of the lamps, along with their ornate ironwork, are survivors from the Victorian era, when more than 40.000 gas lamps lit up the city's pavements in a soft glow. The 200-year-old street lights are mainly in Westminster. Some of the oldest can be spotted on Birdcage Walk by St James's Park.

21 A TINY POLICE STATION

Trafalgar Square
WC2N 5NJ
Covent Garden ①

Okay, so this technically wasn't a police station – there's barely room to fit more than one person inside – but this strange structure in the southeast corner of Trafalgar Square was used by the Metropolitan Police to keep an eye on the comings and goings in the famous London square. The box once had a direct line to Scotland Yard and a light on the top that flashed if there was trouble and an officer was phoning for backup. These days it's no longer in use, though rumour has it Westminster Council uses it as a cleaning cupboard!

22 STRETCHER RAILINGS

AT: LONGLEIGH HOUSE
Peckham Road
SE5 8UW
South ⑫

There is little evidence left of the mark the Blitz made on London – damage was repaired and bomb sites have, for the most part, been built over – but there is one fascinating reminder of that violent period in the city's history that most Londoners have probably never noticed: stretcher railings. These fascinating fences are made up of Air Raid Protection stretchers that were used to carry wounded civilians during World War II. This clever upcycling occurred because after the war there was a large surplus of stretchers and many of London's housing estates had donated their original railings to the war effort. You can still spot them outside Tabard Gardens in Borough and Longleigh House in Peckham, as well as a few other places, mainly south of the river.

22 STRETCHER RAILINGS

23 POLICE POSTS AND BOXES

Aldgate High St
(near St Botolph's)
EC3N 1AB
City of London ②

If you think these blue structures look like something out of *Doctor Who* that's because the time-travelling Tardis was fashioned after a London police box. Their true purpose is a lot less sci-fi. Once commonplace, they were rolled out across London during the late 1920s so patrolling officers and members of the public could contact a local police station. You can spot an example of a traditional police box, based on the original design, outside Earls Court Station, or a handful of the smaller, bright blue police posts, like the one outside St Botolph's Church in Aldgate, around the City. They no longer work, but the cast iron police public call posts are now protected as listed buildings.

24 CABMEN'S SHELTERS

23 Russell Square
WC1H 0XG
Bloomsbury ⑦

London used to be dotted with pretty green huts, no bigger than a horse and cart, that offered shelter to cab drivers across the city. They were built and operated for the drivers of carriages, and later black cabs, after the Cabmen's Shelter Fund charity was established in 1875 – and were basically designed to stop drivers drinking on the job in London's pubs. Drivers would get hot drinks, meals, newspapers and somewhere dry to wait on rainy days in between fares. A handful of these charming huts, like the one in Russell Square, still exist and are still serving up cheap cups of tea and bargain bacon butties to cabbies, as well as members of the public through the takeaway hatches.

Stunning
CEILINGS

---

25 PAINTED HALL
AT: OLD ROYAL NAVAL
COLLEGE
King William Walk
SE10 9NN
South ⑫
+44 (0)20 8269 4747
ornc.org

Even before you've looked up, the Painted Hall is a stunner. It was designed by baroque masters Sir Christopher Wren and Nicholas Hawksmoor and completed in 1727, with elegant window arches and richly decorated walls. The ceiling, adorned with images of monarchs, political alliances and Great Britain's naval powers, is the reason to visit, though. It was painted over 19 years by artist Sir James Thornhill and gazing up at it you can't help but imagine the incredible effort and energy that went into its creation.

26 BANQUETING HOUSE
Whitehall
SW1A 2ER
Westminster ⑤
+44 (0)33 3320 6000
hrp.org.uk/
banqueting-house

Keep your eyes skywards for the Rubens ceiling in Banqueting House, the last remnant of the royal Palace of Whitehall. It's home to the only surviving ceiling painting by artist Sir Peter Paul Rubens. Installed in the hall in 1636, and believed to have been commissioned by King Charles I, the prized canvasses portray *The Union of the Crowns, The Apotheosis of James I* and *The Peaceful Reign of James I*.

27 FITZROVIA CHAPEL
2 Pearson Square
W1T 3BF
Fitzrovia ⑦
+44 (0)20 3409 9895
fitzroviachapel.org

The golden, star-studded and intricately mosaiced ceiling in Fitzrovia Chapel has to be seen to be believed. The chapel, which was once part of Middlesex Hospital, was never consecrated and is open to the public during the day on Wednesdays for quiet reflection and meditation, plus the chance to admire the ornate surroundings.

THE BEATLES
in London

---

28 ABBEY ROAD STUDIOS

3 Abbey Road
NW8 9AY
North ⑭
+44 (0)20 7266 7000
abbeyroad.com/
crossing

Thanks to that 1969 album, which featured all four band members walking across a zebra crossing on Abbey Road, this is probably the most famous Beatles location in the world. The crossing, outside Abbey Road Studios, where the band recorded most of their music, is now a mecca for music fans (and an obstacle for local drivers!). Visit to walk across the road and leave a message on the wall outside the studio.

29 34 MONTAGU SQUARE

W1H 2LJ
Marylebone ⑥

A basement flat a little over a mile away from Abbey Road Studios, 34 Montagu Square was leased by Ringo Starr during the mid-1960s. Paul McCartney rented it from him and is said to have worked on *I'm Looking Through You* and *Eleanor Rigby* there, while another of Ringo's renters, Jimi Hendrix, composed *The Wind Cries Mary* within its walls. John Lennon and Yoko Ono also posed for the nude artwork for their *Two Virgins* album while staying in the flat. Lennon's stay in the property, which is now privately owned and not open to the public, is marked with a blue plaque. Oh, to be a fly on those walls…

30 THE LONDON PALLADIUM

Argyll St
W1F 7TF
Soho ①
+44 (0)20 7087 7755
lwtheatres.co.uk/the-london-palladium

When was the start of 'Beatlemania'? It's said to have been in October 1963, when The Beatles performed at the Palladium, one of London's most famous theatres. Appearing as part of Sunday Night at the London Palladium, a show which was broadcast on telly and watched by millions, the Fab Four played *She Loves You* and *Twist and Shout* before leaving the building to be greeted by heaving crowds of screaming fans. Stand outside on Argyll Street, just off Oxford Street, and imagine the mayhem.

31 THE BRITISH LIBRARY

96 Euston Road
NW1 2DB
King's Cross ⑦
+44 (0)33 0333 1144
bl.uk

The largest national library in the world, The British Library's collection is made up of more than 170 million items, including some priceless Beatles material. Head to the Treasures Gallery to find early drafts of lyrics to *Strawberry Fields Forever*, *She Said She Said* and *In My Life* handwritten by Lennon, alongside other unique treasures like the Magna Carta and original Shakespeare folios.

32 THE CITY BARGE

27 Strand-on-the-Green
W4 3PH
West ⑬
+44 (0)20 8994 2148
citybargechiswick.com

This pub in Chiswick is teeming with history – there's been a riverside boozer on this spot since the 14th century – but it's more famous for its recent past. The pub was used as a filming location in The Beatles' 1965 film *Help!*. Pop inside to order "Two lagers and lime and two lagers and lime", Ringo-style. Then, grab one of the benches on the path out front and enjoy this pub's pretty, Thames-side setting.

Homes with
STAR-STUDDED *histories*

---

33 40 STANSFIELD ROAD

SW9 9RY

South ⑫

David Bowie was one of the world's most successful superstars, but his childhood home was a modest terraced house in Brixton. It's privately owned and there's nothing there to mark it out, but that doesn't stop fans visiting to take a look at where the performer spent his early years. While you're in the area, take a look at the colourful Bowie mural on Brixton Road, opposite the Tube's exit.

34 153 CROMWELL ROAD

SW5 0TQ

Kensington ④

British-born film director Alfred Hitchcock called this smart West London house home for a short time in the 1920s. Before his huge Hollywood success, Hitchcock lived in a quiet corner of Earls Court, in a top floor flat, with his then-new wife Alma. The place is marked with an English Heritage blue plaque.

35 34 PARADISE ROAD

TW9 1SE

West ⑬

A symmetrical, wisteria-fronted house in the centre of riverside Richmond, 34 Paradise Road, also known as Hogarth House, is where Virginia and Leonard Woolf lived between 1915 and 1924. It's where they founded their publishing house Hogarth Press, so named after – you guessed it – their home, in 1917. They began hand-printing books there in the dining room, and the press ended up publishing volumes such as *The Wasteland* by T.S. Eliot, *The Standard Edition of the Complete Psychological Works of Sigmund Freud* and Woolf's own *A Room of One's Own*.

36 3 CHALCOT SQUARE

NW1 8YB
North ⑭

This achingly pretty corner of London boasts a blue plaque marking it out as the home of writer Sylvia Plath. 3 Chalcot Square, one in a row of technicolour townhouses, was where Plath lived with her husband Ted Hughes from 1960-1. In their top floor flat, Plath penned her novel *The Bell Jar* and had her first volume of poetry published. She also lived and died in nearby 23 Fitzroy Road. This address also has a blue plaque, but not because of its connection to Plath – it was the childhood home of poet W.B. Yeats.

37 24 CHESTER SQUARE

SW1W 9HS
Belgravia ⑤

You might imagine the author of a novel like *Frankenstein* would spend her final years somewhere dark and atmospheric. But 24 Chester Square is far from gothic. This grand white town-house on an elegant Belgravia square is where writer Mary Shelley lived and worked between 1846-1851, after a turbulent and tragedy-studded life spent roaming around Europe. It was also here that she passed away on February 1, 1851.

38 102 EDITH GROVE

SW10 0NH
Chelsea ④

There's no blue plaque marking this terrace just off King's Road, but a bedsit on Edith Grove was the place Mick Jagger, Keith Richards and Brian Jones called home in the early 1960s during the early days of The Rolling Stones.

Historic
BOATS

39 WORD ON THE WATER

Regent's Canal Towpath (near Granary Square) N1C 4BZ King's Cross ⑦

Word on the Water is a floating bookshop that calls a 100-year-old Dutch canal boat home. Stop by to pick up your next novel, listen to a book reading or, in the winter months, cosy up next to the water-borne wood burner. You can find the vintage book barge bobbing on Regent's Canal, near Granary Square – a former canal basin turned food and drink hub – and Coal Drops Yard – a hip shopping district in restored Victorian railway arches.

39 WORD ON THE WATER

40 CUTTY SARK

King William Walk
SE10 9HT
South ⑫
+44 (0)20 8312 6608
rmg.co.uk/cutty-sark

Perched in an iron and glass cradle beside the river in Greenwich, *Cutty Sark* is an elegant, nautical time capsule. The former tea clipper, built in 1869, was once one of the fastest and finest to ride the waves. The sailing boat used to transport tea across the sea from China to London, and bring Australian wool across the globe to Britain. Now you can wander the historic deck and even stand underneath the boat's copper hull.

41 HMS BELFAST

The Queen's Walk
SE1 2JH
South Bank ③
+44 (0)20 7416 5000
*iwm.org.uk/
hms-belfast*

HMS Belfast is an imposing warship sitting on the river Thames in the shadow of Tower Bridge – but its presence in central London is far from ominous. The enormous ship, which is a survivor of WWII, is permanently moored there as a museum. There's something surreal about exploring the nine, weapon-laden decks of this battleship, one of only three that survives from the D-Day bombardment fleet, while modern-day London life continues on around you.

42 THE GOLDEN HINDE

Cathedral St
SE1 9DE
South Bank ③
+44 (0)20 7403 0123
goldenhinde.co.uk

Captained by Elizabethan explorer Sir Francis Drake in the 16th century, *The Golden Hinde* was famous for being the first English ship to circumnavigate the globe. The black, red and gold vessel that can be found along the South Bank is pretty convincing, but this boat is actually a replica. The original rotted in a Deptford dockyard, with the best bits of timber being used to make a chair that can be seen today at The Bodleian Library in Oxford. This ship, which opens to visitors daily, was given life in the 1970s using traditional techniques to keep it as similar to Drake's resilient ship as possible.

Places with
VINTAGE VIBES

―――――――

43 CAHOOTS

13 Kingly Court
W1B 5PW
Soho ①
+44 (0)20 7352 6200
cahoots-london.com

Be transported to London during the 1940s at clever, themed bar Cahoots. It purports to be inside an old Tube station, and the stunning interiors will almost have you convinced. Expect theatrics, costumes, vintage decor and retro tunes, as well as a cocktail menu printed on newspapers. Book a seat inside the old Tube carriage for a jolly good time – it's the only place you're allowed to drink on the London Underground.

44 POPPIE'S FISH & CHIPS

6-8 Hanbury St
E1 6QR
Spitalfields ⑨
+44 (0)20 7247 0892
*poppies
fishandchips.co.uk*

This retro-style fish and chip shop, with its music hall melodies and staff in vintage uniforms, harks back to the 1950s, when owner Pat 'Pop' Newland first started working in the batter business. Order classic East End fare like jellied eels and saveloys as well as delicious, ethically sourced fish and piping hot chips. There are also branches in Soho and Camden.

45 BOBBY FITZPATRICK

273 West End Lane
NW6 1QS
North ⑭
+44 (0)20 7433 1989
bobbyf.co.uk

You'll have a thing for retro tiling after a drink or two at Bobby Fitzpatrick. The 1970s-themed bar is clad in a wonderful array of bold and clashing patterns in muted shades. Feeling groovy? You will be when you're sipping something punchy in a rattan chair beneath a macramé plant hanger.

46 MAGGIE'S CLUB

329 Fulham Road
SW10 9QL
Chelsea ④
+44 (0)20 7352 8512
maggies-club.com

If the 1980s are your jam, you'll love the vibe at Maggie's where the tables are Rubik's cubes, hair is permed and Margaret Thatcher speeches are streamed in the loos. If it appeals, you can even drink cocktails out of the former prime minister's head, while back-to-back 1980s hits blast out in the background.

47 LITTLE NAN'S BAR

AT: DEPTFORD MARKET YD
Arches 13-15
SE8 4BX
South ⑫
+44 (0)77 9220 5375
littlenans.co.uk

You can make yourself right at home at Little Nan's, a joyful bar the owner set up in honour of his late grandma Jojo. The Deptford location (Little Nan's also has outposts in Fitzrovia and Stockwell) is a retro living room in a railway arch, stuffed full of quirky vintage memorabilia, like Princess Diana books, framed photos of former soap stars and novelty knick-knacks. Order sweet cocktails and soak up the silliness.

48 MR FOGG'S TAVERN

58 St Martin's Lane
WC2N 4EA
Covent Garden ①
+44 (0)20 7581 3992
mr-foggs.com

In London it feels like you're never more than a street away from an old pub, but if you're after something a little more immersive, pop into Mr Fogg's Tavern. This Victorian-style boozer, inspired by Jules Verne's novel *Around the World in 80 Days*, is decked out in a changing array of bunting and aging curios. Drinks are served in tankards by staff wearing period aprons and hats, while group sing-alongs are strongly encouraged.

STATUES

that tell a story

49 **MARY SEACOLE**
  Lambeth
  SE1 7GA
  South Bank ③

Standing defiantly outside St Thomas's hospital, on the banks of the Thames and facing the Houses of Parliament, you'll find the likeness of Mary Seacole, a Jamaican-born nurse who cared for wounded British soldiers during the Crimean War in the 19th century. When the statue, by artist Martin Jennings, was unveiled in 2016, it was the first public statue of a named black woman to be erected in the UK.

50 **NATIONAL FIREFIGHTERS MEMORIAL**
  St Paul's Churchyard
  EC4M 8BX
  City of London ②
  firefighters memorial.org.uk

These three bronze figures in Carter Lane Gardens represent firefighters tackling blazes during the Blitz, when huge swathes of London burned after intense bombing. First put on display in the early 1990s, it's since been turned into a national monument, remembering all firefighters who have died in the line of duty. The plinth features the names of all those who have been killed in peacetime.

51 **MILLICENT FAWCETT**
  Parliament Square
  SW1P 3BD
  Westminster ⑤

After months of campaigning, led by activist Caroline Criado Perez, the first statue of a woman was welcomed into Parliament Square in 2018. The artwork from Gillian Wearing depicts suffragette Millicent Fawcett holding a banner which reads 'courage calls to courage everywhere' and was commissioned to mark the 100-year anniversary of the Representation of the People Act, which gave some women over 30 the vote.

COURAGE CALLS TO COURAGE EVERYWHERE

51. MILLICENT FAWCETT

אנכי ה'
לא יהיה
לא תשא
זכור את
כבד את
לא תרצח
לא תנאף
לא תגנב
לא תענה
לא תחמד

Ancient
PLACES OF WORSHIP

52 BEVIS MARKS SYNAGOGUE

4 Heneage Lane
EC3A 5DQ
City of London ②
+44 (0)20 7621 1188
sephardi.org.uk/
bevis-marks

This peaceful and beautiful synagogue, the oldest in the
UK and the only one in Europe to have been in continuous
use for more than 300 years, was built in 1701 and remains
virtually unchanged to this day. It's in a secluded courtyard,
surrounded by modern skyscrapers like The Gherkin, which
were built after much of the local area was destroyed in an
IRA bombing. You can pay a small ticket price to explore
the space most days of the week, while tours are run on
Wednesdays, Fridays and Sundays.

53 ST PANCRAS OLD CHURCH

Pancras Road
NW1 1UL
King's Cross ⑦
+44 (0)20 7424 0724
posp.co.uk/st-pancras-
old-church

There are layers of history to be unearthed in this pretty
church. What stands today was restored and reconstructed
in 1847 after a period of dereliction, yet the church claims to
be able to trace its history 'at least as far back as the Norman
Conquest' and Roman tiles are said to have been found
in the tower. Most intriguing, though, is next door in the
graveyard, where, among others, architect Sir John Soane and
Mary Wollstonecraft, who many consider to be Britain's first
feminist, are buried. Seek out a tree mysteriously encircled with
old gravestones. During the 1860s, with the expansion of the
railways, a number of bodies had to be exhumed and reburied
elsewhere – and the man tasked with the job decided to arrange
the redundant headstones in a pattern around the base of a
tree. That man happened to be a young Thomas Hardy, who
would go on to write novels like *Tess of the D'Urbervilles*.

54 ST ETHELDREDA'S CHURCH

14 Ely Place
EC1N 6RY
Holborn ⓘ
+44 (0)20 7405 1061
stetheldreda.com

Built in 1250, St Etheldreda's is the oldest Catholic church in England. You can find it on Ely Place, a gated street on land which used to officially be part of Cambridgeshire, because Ely Palace, the private residence of the influential Bishops of Ely, once stood here. The ancient church is now a peaceful place, with open doors most days, but it's had a turbulent history. During Elizabethan times, the crypt was used as a rowdy tavern, while the chapel became a prison and hospital during the Civil War. Nearby Hatton Garden, a street known for selling jewellery and diamonds, was built on what would have once been St Etheldreda's extensive gardens.

55 WESTMINSTER ABBEY

20 Dean's Yard
SW1P 3PA
Westminster ⑤
+44 (0)20 7222 5152
westminster-abbey.org

World-famous for being the location of the wedding of the Duke and Duchess of Cambridge, the funeral of Princess Diana and the coronation of Queen Elizabeth II, as well as all the monarchs who preceded her, Westminster Abbey is an extraordinary place. It was founded in 960, though today's church dates from 1245, and once you step inside the history that surrounds you is overwhelming. You can wander past the final resting places of Elizabeth I, her half-sister Mary I and Mary Queen of Scots, King Henry V, Charles Dickens and Laurence Olivier. Don't miss the Queen's Diamond Jubilee Galleries, a medieval space high above the Abbey floor, or the Cloisters, where you can have a moment of stillness away from the crowds and really get a sense of the building's hallowed history.

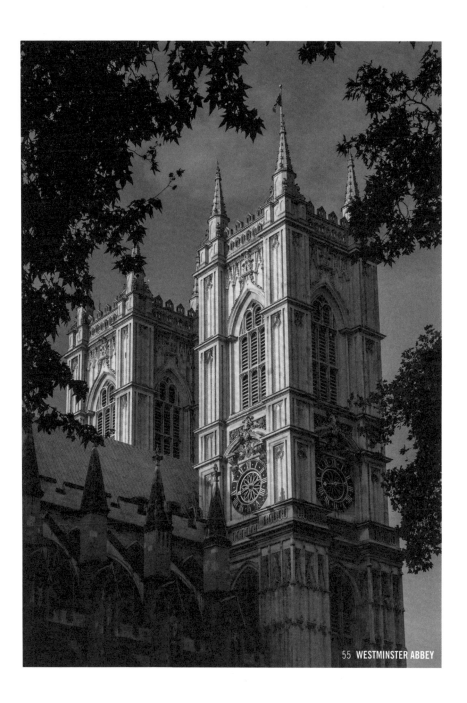

56 ST PAUL'S CATHEDRAL

St Paul's Churchyard
EC4M 8AD
City of London ②
+44 (0)20 7246 8357
stpauls.co.uk

There's been a church on this spot dedicated to St Paul since 604, but the baroque beast that graces the modern London skyline was designed by architect Sir Christopher Wren after its predecessor was destroyed during the Great Fire of London. The new church, complete with iconic dome, took 35 years to build, completing in 1711. Visitors can enjoy a service for free, or, with a sightseeing ticket, gaze at the gorgeous interiors, climb the dome for ace views of the city or have some fun in the Whispering Gallery. The acoustics mean that if you stand on the exact opposite side of the dome as a friend and whisper something, they'll hear you loud and clear, despite being more than 100 feet (30,5 metres) away.

57 ST GILES' WITHOUT CRIPPLEGATE

Fore St
EC2Y 8DA
City of London ②
+44 (0)20 7638 1997
stgilesnewsite.co.uk

Surrounded by the modern buildings of the Barbican Estate, this old church is one of the only medieval churches left standing in London. It survived the Great Fire of 1666 and the Blitz, though was left badly damaged. The building you see today was built in 1394 on the site of an early Saxon church and is so named because at the time its location was outside the City of London's walls at Cripplegate, one of seven gates. *Paradise Lost* writer John Milton was buried there in 1674 and it's also where a young Oliver Cromwell married in 1620. The bright church is normally open in the middle of the day during the week.

58 BRICK LANE MOSQUE

59 Brick Lane
E1 6QL
Spitalfields ⑨
bricklane
jammemasjid.org.uk

On the corner of Fournier Street and Brick Lane stands a Georgian building with a varied history. Now the Brick Lane Jamme Masjid, it's a spiritual hub for local Muslims and not a tourist attraction, but it captures how the rich character of this corner of East London has changed over the centuries. Built in 1743, it was first a French Protestant Church serving the Huguenots who settled in Spitalfields. Then, in the 1890s, the space was turned into a synagogue for the increasing number of Jews who had arrived in the area, before it became a mosque in 1976.

ROMAN
artefacts

---

59 LONDON WALL

Tower Hill
EC3N 4DJ
City of London ②
english-heritage.org.
uk/visit/places/
london-wall

Around 200 AD, there was a strong stone wall, around two and a half miles (four kilometres) long, that wrapped itself around what was then the Roman city of Londinium. Despite all that has changed in the intervening years, sections of that original wall still stand. One of the best places to see it is right by Tower Hill station, where you can spot a tall fragment of the Roman wall, reinforced with medieval brickwork. Afterwards, walk through the City along the route of the ancient wall. Some parts are lost or buried, but there are some well-preserved sections by the Museum of London and on Noble Street where you can get up close with the fascinating ruins.

60 THE MITHRAEUM

12 Walbrook
EC4N 8AA
City of London ②
londonmithraeum.com

The remains of this Roman temple, deep beneath the City of London, were totally lost to history until the construction of an East London office building in 1954. An excavation followed and this mysterious temple, erected by the male worshippers of the god Mithras, was uncovered. Astonishingly, the temple was then moved and inaccurately reconstructed nearby in a car park, but it's back on its original site now and has been painstakingly rebuilt. See some of the treasures this ancient part of London has offered up and explore the atmospheric temple, which uses light and sound to evoke a sense of what it might have been like in Roman times, in this small, free exhibit.

61 LONDON'S ROMAN AMPHITHEATRE

AT: GUILDHALL
ART GALLERY
Guildhall Yard
EC2V 5AE
City of London ②
+44 (0)20 7332 3700
cityoflondon.gov.uk

Under the ancient Guildhall in the City of London is an even older secret: the ruins of a Roman arena. A stretch of stone tunnel, a gate and arena walls were discovered in 1988 as part of an architectural dig in preparation for the building of Guildhall Art Gallery. Back then, Londoners would have sat on tiered benches to watch gruesome gladiatorial games, wild animal fights and the execution of criminals. The Amphitheatre is free to see and open daily beneath the art gallery.

62 BILLINGSGATE ROMAN HOUSE & BATHS

101 Lower Thames St
EC3R 6DL
City of London ②
cityoflondonguides.com

Most citizens of Londinium couldn't afford their own private bath, so they washed in public bathhouses. The remains of one of these can be found hidden beneath office buildings in the City. These rare ruins were discovered in 1848 during the construction of the Coal Exchange and they remain on display in the building's basement. You can discover more about Roman washing habits, and these fascinating foundations, by booking on to a guided tour.

63 TOMB OF THE UNKNOWN LONDON GIRL

30 St Mary Axe
(The Gherkin)
EC3A 8BF
City of London ②

A poignant reminder of the City's ancient past can be found at the base of one of its most modern buildings. During the building of The Gherkin, the skeleton of a teenage girl, estimated to have been buried between 350 and 400 AD, was discovered. Once the work was completed, she was laid back to rest in her original grave. Her final resting place is now marked with an inscribed marble bench and a slab decorated with a laurel wreath. You will find the memorial on the Bury Street side of The Gherkin.

Long-running
EVENTS

---

64 NOTTING HILL CARNIVAL

+44 (0)20 7221 9700
nhcarnival.org

Europe's biggest street festival is far from old-fashioned – Notting Hill Carnival celebrates and showcases London's rich and modern multiculturalism – but the yearly celebration of London's Caribbean communities, their culture and traditions has been taking place outdoors, on the streets of West London, since 1966. It's a colourful, diverse, intense and thrilling spectacle, taking place over two days in August and featuring a parade, mas bands, sound systems, live performances, a whole lot of delicious food and a pulsating mass of partygoers.

65 THE BOAT RACE

theboatrace.org

Every spring Londoners take to the sides of the Thames to watch rowing teams from the historic Universities of Oxford and Cambridge go head to head. The race first took place on 10 June 1829 at Henley-on-Thames after two friends from the opposing universities decided to set up the challenge. Oxford won the initial race and it moved to London and became an annual event around 25 years later. Now the event is televised, or you can go and watch it live from the banks of the river, from Putney to Mortlake, where there's a real party atmosphere, whatever the result.

66 LORD MAYOR'S SHOW

City of London
lordmayorsshow.london

Every autumn the City is inundated with medieval-style pageantry when the new Lord Mayor of London takes office. It's happened for more than 800 years. The day after they are sworn in, the newly elected Lord Mayor parades through the streets of the city in an ancient gilded coach, from Guildhall to the Royal Courts of Justice, to swear loyalty to the crown. The Mayor is joined by carriages, floats, bands and street performers. It's a unique mix of modern and traditional festivities, and a great free day out in the capital.

67 THE PROMS

AT: ROYAL ALBERT HALL
Kensington Gore
SW7 2AP
Kensington ④
+44 (0)20 7589 8212
bbc.co.uk/proms

Get ready to wave your Union Jack – it's practically compulsory at the Last Night of the Proms. This final evening at the Royal Albert Hall is the rousing, theatrical conclusion to an eight-week season of classical concerts. The Proms have been a part of summer in London since 1895, when they were created as an affordable and informal celebration of classical music. These days you can expect free and cheap tickets to hear anything from traditional concert orchestras to soundtracks and scores from iconic movies, at the Royal Albert Hall and other venues around the city.

68 CHANGING THE GUARD

AT: BUCKINGHAM PALACE
SW1A 1AA
St James's ⑤
*household
division.org.uk*

The ceremonial changing of the guards outside Buckingham Palace is one of London's most well-known events. Soldiers have guarded the monarch and the Royal Palaces since 1660, and the ceremony, which takes place when the soldiers currently on duty are replaced by new guards, still happens daily from 10.30 am (11 am on Sundays) and lasts for around an hour. They march, in their iconic red tunics and black hats, accompanied by a full military band, between Buckingham Palace and Wellington Barracks. The key to the palace and responsibility for protecting the Queen is then passed over.

69 LAMBETH COUNTRY SHOW

AT: BROCKWELL PARK

Dulwich Road
SE24 0PA
South ⑫
+44 (0)20 7926 7085
*lambeth
countryshow.co.uk*

Craving some wholesome, old-fashioned vibes? Lambeth Country Show, which has been running for more than 45 years, is a little taste of rural tradition in the city. There are horticultural, livestock and flower shows, plus scarecrow and homegrown vegetable competitions. Don't miss the vegetable-carving competition, which sees people get super-creative with topical and satirical sculptures made out of fruit and veg. It's a grape day out.

70 WIMBLEDON TENNIS CHAMPIONSHIPS

AT: THE ALL ENGLAND LAWN TENNIS CLUB

Church Road
SW19 5AE
Wimbledon ⑬
+44 (0)20 8944 1066
wimbledon.com

Almost certainly the most famous tennis competition in the world, Wimbledon has been taking place in a corner of south-west London at the All England Club since 1877. Then, the game was played to small crowds with just 22 competitors. It's grown in popularity over the years to become the prestigious, world-class event it is today, but many of the rules and traditions remain intact, like the players' almost-entirely-white outfits and the spectators' appetite for strawberries and cream.

64 NOTTING HILL CARNIVAL

ST DUNSTAN IN THE EAST

PLACES

GREEN SPACES

with unusual pasts

71 **PARKLAND WALK**

Florence Road
N4 3EY
North ⑭
+44 (0)20 7527 4374
parkland-walk.org.uk

London's longest nature reserve is a dreamy place for a spot of peace and quiet in North London. Set along an old abandoned railway line, which once ran between Finsbury Park and Alexandra Palace, the walking and cycling trail is surprisingly lush and abundant in wildlife. At Crouch End, you can even walk along the old train platforms, now overgrown with wildflowers.

71 PARKLAND WALK

72 CHELSEA PHYSIC GARDEN

66 Royal Hospital Rd
SW3 4HS
Chelsea ④
+44 (0)20 7352 5646
*chelseaphysic
garden.co.uk*

The oldest botanic garden in London, Chelsea Physic Garden has been in the same spot beside the Thames since 1673. The Worshipful Society of Apothecaries chose their Chelsea site for its riverside, south-facing location, and it served them well – all these years later the garden is home to a thriving collection of around 5000 edible and medicinal plants. Visit early in the year as the garden heralds in the first signs of spring with a snowdrop trail, or to take part in talks and workshops on subjects like growing your own food and using herbs to aid sleep.

73 POSTMAN'S PARK

King Edward St
EC1A 7BT
City of London ②
+44 (0)20 7374 4127
cityoflondon.gov.uk

This inner-city space is a popular spot for lunch-breaking Londoners, but there's more to this park than its shady benches. It's where you'll find the Watts Memorial to Heroic Self-Sacrifice, which was built in 1900 by George Frederick Watts, a Victorian painter and philanthropist. The memorial is made up of 54 ceramic tablets, commemorating 62 Londoners who died trying to save the life of another. Their desperate tales make for moving reading.

74 HILL GARDEN AND PERGOLA

North End Way
NW3 7EX
North ⑭
+44 (0)20 7332 3322
cityoflondon.gov.uk

Hampstead Heath is known for its wide, wild greenery and natural vistas – it's like a little piece of the countryside in the middle of the city – but there's man-made beauty to be found nearby, too. Built by Lord Leverhulme in 1905, on a hill constructed using soil dug out during an extension to the Tube tunnels, the Pergola is a gorgeous Georgian terrace, made up of walkways, trellises, pillars and archways. By the time it was taken over by London City Council in the 1960s and opened to the public, the Pergola was dilapidated and overrun with climbing plants. It's been restored a little since then, but is still romantically run down. Stroll along its faded grandeur and it's easy to picture the extravagant garden parties that once took place here.

75 ST JAMES'S PARK

SW1A 2BJ
St James's ⑤
+44 (0)30 0061 2350
royalparks.org.uk

Not just a great place to eat your sandwiches, St James's Park used to be a marshy water meadow used by Queen Elizabeth I for extravagant fetes before King Charles II opened it up as a public green space. The pretty patch in front of Buckingham Palace is still home to a handful of pelicans, who were introduced to the park in 1664 as a gift from the Russian ambassador. They are free to roam so you might end up sharing a bench with one. If not, to ensure you catch sight of them, head to Duck Island Cottage where the birds are fed a fresh fish lunch every afternoon.

76 KING HENRY'S MOUND

Queen's Road
TW10 5HX
West ⑬
+44 (0)30 0061 2200
royalparks.org.uk

Richmond has loads of royal connections. King Henry VII built a palace there (the remains of the gatehouse can be found just off Richmond Green), while Charles I was responsible for turning the wild landscape into the walled deer park that became Richmond Park. There's also King Henry's Mound, said to be the spot where Henry VIII stood, waiting for a signal from the Tower of London that would tell him his wife Anne Boleyn had been executed and he was free to marry again. The story is unlikely to be true, but it's still worth a visit for the views. The vista from here to St Paul's Cathedral is protected, and when you're standing, surrounded by greenery, and looking towards the city in the distance, you'll be glad it is.

77 GREENWICH PARK

SE10 8QY
South ⑫
+44 (0)30 0061 2381
royalparks.org.uk

This isn't your average city park – Greenwich Park is home to the prime meridian, an imaginary line running from the north to the south pole. Since 1884, every single place on Earth has been measured in terms of its angle east or west from this line. It's also the centre of world time; before GMT (Greenwich Mean Time) was established, there were no international rules about how hours, minutes or days were measured. Visit the Royal Observatory in Greenwich Park to straddle a physical line on the courtyard floor which marks the meridian line... Or, head 102 metres east into the park itself which, thanks to advanced technology, we now know is the true location of 0 degrees longitude.

74 HILL GARDEN AND PERGOLA

Romantic
RUINS

78 ST DUNSTAN IN THE EAST

St Dunstan's Hill
EC3R 5DD
City of London ②
+44 (0)20 7374 4127
cityoflondon.gov.uk

Finding this quiet spot, just minutes away from the City and the Tower of London, feels like you've stumbled across a secret. Grade I-listed church St Dunstan in the East was originally built around 1100. When it was damaged during the Great Fire of London, it was patched up and architect Sir Christopher Wren added a steeple and a tower. The church was badly damaged once again during the Blitz in 1941, but the decision was made not to restore or rebuild it. Instead it's become a secluded and achingly pretty public garden, where plants climb around the remains of the church's glassless windows.

79 CRYSTAL PALACE

Thicket Road
SE20 8DT
South ⑫
*crystalpalace
park.org.uk*

An enormous glass palace once stood on this spot, which is now known as Crystal Palace Park. Originally constructed in Hyde Park in 1851 to house the Great Exhibition, the palace moved, glass panel by glass panel, over the river once the world-famous fair was finished. For a time it housed exhibitions, concerts and circuses, but the elaborate palace sadly fell into disrepair and was destroyed by a fire in 1936. You can still spot foundation stones, terraces, stairs, headless figures and sphinx statues in the park, as well as a series of 'life-size' (and now proven to be anatomically incorrect) Victorian dinosaurs in the greenery.

80 CHRIST CHURCH GREYFRIARS

King Edward St
EC1A 7BA
City of London ②
cityoflondon.gov.uk

You'll find fragrant roses and climbing towers of flowers in the ruins of this ancient church. The body of the church, built on the site of the 1225 Franciscan church of Greyfriars, was destroyed by incendiary bombs in 1940. Now, it's a pretty garden in the shadow of the one remaining tower, designed to reflect the floor plan of the original church, with flower beds sitting where pews once did.

81 WINCHESTER PALACE

Clink St
SE1 9DG
South Bank ③
+44 (0)37 0333 1181
english-heritage.org.uk/
visit/places/winchester-
palace

You could easily walk right by the ruins of Winchester Palace, but it was one of the most important buildings in medieval London. Built in the early 13th century, the riverside palace was the London residence of the powerful bishops of Winchester. All you'll find left today is a few sections of wall, one inset with a beautiful rose window, that were once part of the great hall.

82 ST GEORGE'S GARRISON CHURCH

South Circular A205
SE18 6XJ
South ⑫
stgeorgeswoolwich.org

Originally built in the 1860s to serve the Royal Artillery in Woolwich, St George's Garrison Church was a grand local landmark, designed in Italian-Romanesque style with richly decorated interiors, bold mosaics and stained glass. After being bombed in World War II and partially destroyed, the ruins became a memorial garden, with a modern roof protecting what remains of the church's impressive interior. It's open to the public every Sunday.

83 ASYLUM CHAPEL

AT: CAROLINE GARDENS
Asylum Road
SE15 2SQ
South ⑫
+44 (0)20 7635 8033
maverickprojects.co.uk/
asylum

Built in the early 1800s, at the heart of a complex of almshouses which housed eldery and impoverished pub landlords, Asylum Chapel was at one time the heart of the local community. After being bombed in the Blitz, the chapel and its stained-glass windows, which miraculously survived, were stabilised and made watertight but the building was left derelict. Nowadays it is a popular wedding venue and events space thanks to its unusual and atmospheric interior.

Crumbling
CEMETERIES

---

84 HIGHGATE CEMETERY

Swain's Lane
N6 6PJ
North ⑭
+44 (0)20 8340 1834
highgatecemetery.org

It might not seem like an obvious place for a day out, but Highgate Cemetery really is a must-visit. It opened in 1839 as one of London's Magnificent Seven – grand, private Victorian cemeteries built outside central London at a time when the city was running out of space for its dead and grave robbing from overcrowded churchyards was rife. After more than a century, profits started to wane, graves began to crumble and become smothered by greenery, and the woodland cemetery was declared bankrupt in 1960. The Friends of Highgate Cemetery now care for the gloriously gothic burial ground – and attempt to keep the creeping ivy at bay. For a small entrance fee you can show yourself around the East Cemetery, which is the final resting place of famous figures such as Karl Marx, poet Christina Rossetti and writer George Eliot. The West Cemetery, with its steep trails, impressive architecture and grand catacombs, is accessible via guided tour only.

85 KENSAL GREEN CEMETERY

Harrow Road
W10 4RA
West ⑬
+44 (0)20 8969 0152
*kensalgreen
cemetery.com*

The first of the Magnificent Seven commercial burial grounds, Kensal Green opened in 1833. The garden cemetery's 72 acres, which border the Grand Union Canal, are still in use today for burials of people from all faiths. It's also open to the public. Go to spot stunning funerary monuments or the local wildlife that has made a home in the green space. You can visit on any day of the year or book one of the regular Friends of Kensal Green Cemetery tours.

86 BROMPTON CEMETERY

Fulham Road
SW10 9UG
Chelsea ④
+44 (0)20 7352 1201
royalparks.org.uk

Grade I-listed Brompton Cemetery, another of the magnificent Victorian cemeteries, makes a picturesque place to explore, with imposing buildings and grand walkways lined with trees. It was designed to be a public garden as well as a burial space, and these days it still is, boasting a buzzy cafe and a busy events calendar – film screenings, mindfulness workshops, exhibitions and performances have all taken place within the cemetery, which is free and open daily.

87 TOWER HAMLETS CEMETERY

Southern Grove
E3 4PX
East ⑬
+44 (0)20 8983 1277
fothcp.org

Once an elegant burial ground, Tower Hamlets Cemetery suffered from neglect and was further damaged during bombing raids in World War II. The space officially became a wild and peaceful public nature reserve in 1966. There are still graves and monuments to be found here – it is the final resting place of more than 350.000 people – but the cemetery now resembles a natural woodland. The Friends of Tower Hamlets Cemetery Park run conservation and heritage volunteering events as well as festivals, talks and workshops.

88 WEST NORWOOD CEMETERY

Norwood Road
SE27 9JU
South ⑫
+44 (0)20 7926 7999
westnorwood cemetery.org

This Gothic-style, Victorian cemetery is open for visitors every day, while Friends of West Norwood Cemetery run free tours on the first Sunday of each month. The cemetery also runs events itself, like slow flow yoga classes, meditation sessions and suitably creepy bat walks at twilight. The burial ground certainly makes a stunning setting. 65 of the cemetery's monuments are listed, while notable plots include a grand terracotta mausoleum for Sir Henry Doulton, the famous pottery manufacturer, another for Sir Henry Tate, the founder of the Tate art galleries, and a simple headstone for well-known Victorian cookery writer Mrs Beeton.

Historic
MARKETS

---

89 COLUMBIA ROAD MARKET

Columbia Road
E2 7RG
East ⑬
columbiaroad.info

The weekly frenzy of flowers and foliage on Columbia Road is a modern-day Instagrammer's dream, but the market has roots in the 19th century. Wealthy philanthropist Angela Burdett-Coutts established Columbia Market in 1868 as a grand, covered food market to serve the poor in what was then a deprived area of the East End. It's changed a lot over the years – it's now a Sunday flower market – but stalls are still selling in the same spot. Visit early to stock up on seasonal flowers and plants before the crowds descend – or wait until 3 pm, when everything starts to wind down, to buy armfuls of blooms at bargain prices.

90 BOROUGH MARKET

8 Southwark St
SE1 1TL
South Bank ③
+44 (0)20 7407 1002
boroughmarket.org.uk

The best and most famous food market in London is also one of the city's oldest. Borough Market, which now sits in the shadow of the ultra-modern Shard, has been on or near this site for more than 1000 years. The spot, on the southside of the Thames, has been a hive of activity for centuries. As the city has changed so has Borough, from the chaos of the unregulated medieval market to the artisan food hub it is today. Eating your way around the stalls, beneath the market's Victorian ironwork, is one of the greatest ways to spend an afternoon in London. Don't miss Monmouth for ace coffee, Brindisa for Spanish treats or Kappacasein for dreamy cheese toasties.

91 SMITHFIELD MARKET

Charterhouse St
EC1A 9PS
City of London ②
+44 (0)20 7248 3151
smithfieldmarket.com

Smithfield Market is the biggest – and oldest – wholesale meat market in the country. It's been trading on the same site since the late Middle Ages. Then, it was in a big open space outside the city's boundaries, but these days the market, and the grand Grade II-listed buildings it calls home, is right in the middle of the action, surrounded by highrises and office blocks. It might not be the case for much longer though, as there are plans to move Smithfield out of London. Explore the market or take a tour while you still can – and if you can cope with the early start. Smithfield Market is open to all from 2 am Monday to Friday.

92 COVENT GARDEN MARKET

AT: THE MARKET BUILDING
WC2E 8RF
Covent Garden ①
+44 (0)20 7420 5856
coventgarden.london

Covent Garden is famous for its street performers and the high-end shops, cafes and bars that attract tourist crowds, but the area has a fascinating history. The Italian-style, pedestrianised piazza was designed by famous architect Inigo Jones in the 17th century, while the stunning Greco-Roman market building was built in 1828 by architect Charles Fowler to house the rowdy fruit and veg market that had popped up in the heart of the square. A later addition, the Flower Market Building, is now the London Transport Museum, while Fowler's airy, colonnaded construction remains a buzzing market to this day, with permanent stores in the arches.

93 OLD SPITALFIELDS MARKET

16 Horner Square
E1 6EW
Spitalfields ⑨
oldspitalfields
market.com

There's been a market on this site in East London for hundreds of years. It's grown and grown since the 17th century, with the cavernous Victorian structure and neat, terraced frontage you can see today being built in the late 1800s. What you can buy here has changed – the fruit and veg market moved out to Leyton in the 1990s, being replaced with art, antiques, vinyl and design stores and stalls – but the place retains a nostalgic charm that's hard to beat.

Ancient **ALLEYWAYS** and **PASSAGES**

94 GOODWIN'S COURT

WC2N 4LL
Covent Garden ①

Wander down Goodwin's Court and it's hard to imagine you're still just a few steps away from the bright lights of Leicester Square. Lit by old-fashioned gas lamps, the narrow court is lined with neat, glossy black doors and curved windows right out of the 17th century. The terrace has hardly changed over the centuries, evoking the sense that you've just stumbled into the pages of a Dickens novel.

95 BRYDGES PLACE

WC2N 4HP
Covent Garden ①

It might not be the most attractive alleyway in London, but this slim stretch of footpath that runs alongside the Colosseum, between St Martin's Lane and Bedfordbury, is one of London's tiniest. It measures in at around 34 inches at its narrowest point. Go squeeze along this little passageway to feel like you've stepped back in time – and to avoid those packed pavements!

96 NEAL'S YARD

WC2H 9DP
Covent Garden ①
nealsyardlondon.co.uk

Populated with alternative therapy studios, trendy cafes and hippy health food restaurants, Neal's Yard is a technicolour, greenery-covered gem in Seven Dials. But it wasn't always such a draw. The buildings date back from the 17th century, but the courtyard and its connecting alleyways weren't put on the map until the 1970s when entrepreneur Nicholas Saunders began to transform the pretty much derelict area, which had been used as storage space for the Covent Garden fruit and veg market, into the thriving hub you can discover today.

97 BLEEDING HEART YARD

EC1N 8SJ
Holborn ①

The name of this little cul-de-sac is enough to bring gruesome thoughts of gothic Victorian London to mind, and there are a number of suitably grisly tales about the quiet spot, too. Legend has it the place got its name after the death of Lady Elizabeth Hatton, who was found here, murdered, with her heart still pumping blood out on to the cobbles. While in novel *Little Dorrit*, Charles Dickens recalls "the legend of a young lady of former times closely imprisoned in her chamber by a cruel father for remaining true to her own true love, and refusing to marry the suitor he chose for her... the young lady used to be seen up at her window behind the bars, murmuring a love-lorn song of which the burden was, 'Bleeding heart, bleeding heart, bleeding away,' until she died."

98 PICKERING PLACE

SW1A 1EA
St James's ⑤

A miniscule courtyard in St James's, Pickering Place is said to be the smallest public square in the city. Access to the secluded spot is as atmospheric as London alleyways get (and they're a pretty atmospheric bunch), along a unique wood panelled passageway. Look out for a plaque which captures a very specific moment in time, when the place was the embassy of the then-Republic of Texas between 1842 and 1845.

98 PICKERING PLACE

Magical
MEWS

99 **BATHURST MEWS**

W2 2SB

West ⑬

There's something incredibly nostalgic about London's mews streets. Now super-desirable places to live, the neat terraces and courtyards used to be stables and servants' quarters that served London's large houses. Bathurst Mews, with its cobbles and cute, cookie-cutter homes, is no exception. What makes this spot stand out from the rest is the fact that it's still home to horses. Hyde Park Stables run horse riding lessons from Bathurst Mews, taking riders out into nearby Hyde Park and often along Rotten Row, which has been a popular place to trot since the 18th century.

100 **HOLLAND PARK MEWS**

W11 3SS

Kensington ④

It might have been designed in 1860 as a service street, but Holland Park Mews is pretty grand by today's standards. The rows of houses on either side of the road, with petite proportions and matching iron railed balconies, are Grade II-listed thanks to their 'unusual design' and 'picturesqueness', while the entrance to the mews is marked by a huge stone archway.

101 **ST LUKE'S MEWS**

W11 1DF

West ⑬

The colourful section of buildings between All Saints and St Luke's roads are a charming example of a well-preserved, historic London mews, just a few minutes' walk from Portobello Road. Think you recognise it? That'll be because the street starred in Richard Curtis's movie *Love Actually*.

102 **KYNANCE MEWS**

SW7 4QR
Kensington ④

This might just be the prettiest mews street in the capital. Originating in the 1860s, it's a popular spot with visitors after a perfect snap, and it's easy to see why. The cobbled street is accessed through three protected, stucco arches while buildings are draped in trailing greenery – bold, red leaves in autumn and, in spring, abundantly blooming wisteria.

ROADS
that time forgot

---

103 LITTLE GREEN STREET

NW5 1BL
North ⑭

The Kinks used this spot as the backdrop for their music video *Dead End Street*, but that's not the only reason to visit Little Green Street. Together, the terraced houses on this small lane make up one of the best-preserved Georgian streets in the city. The buildings – eight quaint cottages – have barely changed since the 18th century. Check out the bowed, ground-floor windows, which would have been shopfronts.

104 SHAD THAMES

SE1 2NJ
South Bank ③

You can get a real sense of London's nautical history by strolling down Shad Thames. The riverside street has cobbles underfoot and criss-crossing iron walkways overhead, most linking Butler's Wharf on one side of the street to the Cardamom Building on the other. These industrial buildings, now mainly residential, were part of a thriving warehouse complex – the largest in London during Victorian times – storing goods like spices, tea and coffee that were unloaded from ships docking nearby in the city.

105 ROUPELL STREET

SE1 8TB
South Bank ③

Turn into Roupell Street and it's like you've fallen through time. The neat, two-storey terraces are a totally intact example of what much of London would have looked like in the 19th century, and it feels miraculous that it's all still there, just a few minutes away from large-scale housing developments, Waterloo station and the busy South Bank. Don't miss a wander down the equally lovely Theed Street.

106 FOURNIER STREET

E1 6QE
Spitalfields ⑨

Surrounded by modern development, Fournier Street is a perfectly preserved stretch of dignified 18th-century homes, with delicate window frames and ornate wooden doorcases. Built in the early 1700s to accommodate the French Huguenot silk weavers, who had arrived in the area, they were used as both homes and workshops. The silk for Queen Victoria's coronation gown was woven at number 14. Ignore the double yellows and the modern cars and it's easy to let yourself be transported to another time.

107 LOMBARD STREET

EC3V 9AA
City of London ②

Once the heart of the banking district, this street in the City has changed a fair bit over the years. A little of its history can be revealed by looking at the distinctive signs that hang from Lombard Street's building fronts, though. Put up to mark Edward VII's coronation in 1902, the signs allude to historic businesses that once ran out of Lombard Street.

108 CHEYNE WALK

SW3 5LX
Chelsea ④

Cheyne Walk is a charming riverside street lined with almost untouched Jacobean and Queen Anne-era homes. Right beside the Thames with far-reaching views, it's an enviable spot and has attracted a string of notable residents over the years. The painter J.M.W. Turner spent the last years of his life in number 119, where a young Ian Fleming lived years later. Writers Henry James, T.S. Eliot and George Eliot also lived on the street, as did the Pre-Raphaelite painter Dante Gabriel Rossetti, who resided in number 16, along with a number of exotic animals including an armadillo and a wombat. In 1968, Mick Jagger and Marianne Faithful stayed at number 48, while a year later his bandmate Keith Richards moved into number 3. Both attracted police attention to the Walk, having their homes raided by the drugs squad in the late 1960s and early 1970s.

105 ROUPELL STREET

BARBICAN

BUILDINGS

Glorious
GREENHOUSES

109 TEMPERATE AND PALM HOUSE

AT: KEW ROYAL
BOTANIC GARDENS
TW9 3AE
West ⑬
+44 (0)20 8332 5655
kew.org

Kew Gardens is one of the UK's UNESCO World Heritage Sites thanks to its beautifully maintained historical buildings and landscape, in which garden design and fashions from across the centuries, including work from famous landscape architects, are preserved. A botanical garden established by the royal family, Kew opened to the public in 1840. Today, you can find one of the biggest and most diverse plant collections in the world here, plus acres of lush greenery to wander around. The standout stars, though, are the garden's perfectly preserved Victorian greenhouses. Palm House is humid and tropical inside while Temperate House, the world's largest Victorian glasshouse, is home to 1500 species of plants from the world's temperate zones. Both are total stunners.

110 CHISWICK HOUSE CONSERVATORY

AT: CHISWICK HOUSE
AND GARDENS
Burlington Lane
W4 2RP
West ⑬
+44 (0)20 3141 3350
*chiswickhouseand
gardens.org.uk*

Once one of the largest in the world, the Grade I-listed, 300-foot (91,5-metre) glasshouse in the gardens of Chiswick House has since been dwarfed, but it's still well worth a visit. It was built in the 18th century to house the Duke of Devonshire's impressive collection of camellia plants, and 200 years later it's still doing the same job. Go to spot the 'Middlemist's Red' camellia – it's one of the rarest plants on the planet. Afterwards, explore the rest of the gardens, which include walled kitchen gardens which supply the cafe, a symmetrical Italian garden and huge Atlantic blue cedar trees. The Beatles filmed *Paperback Writer* and *Rain* in these gardens.

111 SYON PARK'S GREAT CONSERVATORY

AT: SYON HOUSE

Syon Park

TW8 8JF

West ⑬

+44 (0)20 8560 0882

syonpark.co.uk

In the grounds of 16th-century Syon House you'll find a well-preserved, delicate glasshouse with a bold, domed roof. It was built in the early 19th century and filled with an array of exotic plants. Visit after dark in the run-up to Christmas to see the conservatory and surrounding parkland illuminated with colourful lights as part of Syon Park's annual Enchanted Woodland trail.

111 SYON PARK'S GREAT CONSERVATORY

Historic
SWIMMING POOLS

112 **BROCKWELL LIDO**

AT: BROCKWELL PARK
Dulwich Road
SE24 0PA
South ⑫
+44 (0)20 7274 3088
fusion-lifestyle.com/
centres/brockwell-lido

Built in 1937, this retro open-air pool in Brockwell Park is a popular swimming spot, and a fine example of pared-back art deco design. The much-loved Grade II-listed landmark has been at the heart of the local community for decades. Its red brick design is virtually changed, although a spa, gym and the must-visit Lido Cafe beside the pool have been added in recent years. You'll also find plenty of activities here that don't require swimming trunks, like a festival of 20th-century design or a screening of classic film *Jaws*.

113 **PORCHESTER SPA**

Queensway
W2 5HS
West ⑬
+44 (0)20 7221 6118
everyoneactive.com/
porchesterspa

Scrub the years away at this unusual Grade II*-listed spa and swimming pool, which dates back to the 1920s. While some facilities have been given a more modern makeover, Porchester Spa retains its retro feel and Victorian-style Turkish Bath layout, with steam rooms, plunge pool and traditional relaxation space. Spot the original green and white tiles from 1929 in the basement's hot rooms, the tepidarium, caldarium and laconium.

114 **CAMBERWELL PUBLIC BATHS**

Artichoke Place
SE5 8TS
South ⑫
+44 (0)20 7703 3024
everyoneactive.com/
centre/camberwell-
leisure-centre

This 19th-century pool is a real beauty, with a vaulted ceiling framing skylights and delicate, original ironwork along the viewing gallery. When it opened in 1891, the Renaissance-style building contained first- and second-class swimming pools – one of which is now boarded over and used as a sports hall – private 'slipper' baths and laundry facilities. It's a modern leisure centre now that still retains a strong sense of its Victorian roots.

115 WILLES POOL

AT: KENTISH TOWN
SPORTS CENTRE
Grafton Road
NW5 3DU
North ⑭
+44 (0)20 7974 7000
better.org.uk/kentish-
town-sports-centre

A bold 1960s renovation had hidden away the stunning Victorian design of this North London pool, which opened as St Pancras Baths in 1903. But thanks to a recent, and more sympathetic, overhaul the building's original features are back on display. Willes Pool is the star attraction. It has an elegant vaulted ceiling studded with roof lights, that throw sunlight down on to the water, and original timber beams, all of which had been obscured by a suspended ceiling. Marvel at it from the wooden public viewing gallery or while you take a dip.

116 MARSHALL STREET BATHS

15 Marshall St
W1F 7EL
Soho ①
+44 (0)20 7734 4325
everyoneactive.com/
centre/marshall-street-
leisure-centre

Splashing around in Soho's historic baths is like travelling back in time. There are all the modern features you'd expect, like a hot yoga studio and a fancy gym, but the real draw is the beautiful Victorian swimming pool, complete with its original 1930s marble floor and dreamy barrel-vaulted ceiling. Spot other timeless features, like the original wooden ticket booth beside the pool.

117 IRONMONGER ROW BATHS

1 Norman St
EC1V 3AA
Islington ⑧
+44 (0)20 3642 5520
better.org.uk/
ironmonger-row-baths

From a public wash house to a leisure centre and spa, the Grade II-listed Ironmonger Row Baths has changed quite a bit since it was built in the 1930s. There are lots of original features to be found, though. Look up at the vintage design and teak seating while you do your backstroke in the pool, or admire the original wooden cubicles in the Turkish spa.

Lovely
LIBRARIES

118 THE LONDON LIBRARY

14 St James's Square
SW1Y 4LG
St James's ⑤
+44 (0)20 7766 4700
londonlibrary.co.uk

Founded in 1841, the London Library has become the largest independent lending library in the world, with more than a million books behind its grand doors. The building it calls home is an intriguing marriage of 19th-century and more modern design. The plush reading room, which was opened in 1896, is all neat columns and elegant cornicing. Many of the books sit on Grade II-listed Victorian stacks with iron-grille floors, while newer additions from the 1930s onwards are simple and sleek. Charles Dickens, Virginia Woolf and Agatha Christie are among the writers to have frequented this historic institution. Membership isn't cheap – the standard full rate is 510 pounds a year – but you can explore the space for free on one of the library's regular evening tours.

119 KENSINGTON CENTRAL LIBRARY

12 Phillimore Walk
W8 7RX
Kensington ④
+44 (0)20 7361 3010
rbkc.gov.uk

The opening of this grand, purpose-built library in 1960 was met with distaste from locals, who thought the classical-style building was an outdated eyesore. You can't help but fall for the neat interior of this library, though, with its well-preserved terrazzo floors, striped square columns, brass and mahogany shelving and stunning hanging clock.

120 SWISS COTTAGE CENTRAL LIBRARY

88 Avenue Road
NW3 3HA
North ⑭
+44 (0)20 7974 4444
camden.gov.uk

In the early 1960s, architect Sir Basil Spence, who was known for his modernist style, designed an unusual and ambitious building for this council-run library – and it's become something of an architectural landmark. Curves and slim lines connect its rounded exterior to its interior, where symmetrical spiral staircases and narrow balustrades draw your eye. Afterwards, visit the nearby Alexandra and Ainsworth Estate for more modernist design.

121 BETHNAL GREEN LIBRARY

Cambridge Heath
Road
E2 0HL
East ⑪
+44 (0)20 7364 3492
ideastore.co.uk/
bethnal-green-library

Bethnal Green's public library first opened in 1922, in a late-Victorian building that was once part of Bethnal House Asylum. The Grade II-listed space was recently renovated, but the original period features remain. Pop in to borrow a bestseller and eye up the classical panelling, checkerboard flooring, curved ceiling and ornamental plasterwork while you're at it.

119 KENSINGTON CENTRAL LIBRARY

Amazing
TRAIN STATIONS

122 ST PANCRAS INTERNATIONAL STATION

Euston Road
N1C 4QP
King's Cross ⑦
+44 (0)20 7843 7688
stpancras.com

With its sweeping wrought iron roof and grand Gothic exterior, St Pancras Station is a brilliant example of Victorian style and engineering. When it was built, the roof was the largest single span roof in the world. The station has changed a lot since it first opened – it now runs Eurostar trains to the continent – but the modern station has been designed to allow its 19th century origins to shine. Wander along the neat red brick arches and allow yourself to be transported back to 1868.

122 ST PANCRAS INTERNATIONAL STATION

123 GANTS HILL UNDERGROUND STATION

Cranbrook Road
IG2 6UD
Ilford

Hundreds of Londoners may well use this gateway to the Central Line every day without ever noticing its unique design, but look up and it's kind of special. Designed by Charles Holden in a simple, modernist style, the 1930s station features a sleek barrel-vaulted ceiling said to have been inspired by the Moscow metro system. Like what you see? Holden also designed stately Senate House, which houses the University of London's library, and 55 Broadway, considered to be the city's first skyscraper.

124 CLAPHAM SOUTH STATION

Balham Hill
SW12 9DU
South ⑫
+44 (0)343 222 5000
ltmuseum.co.uk/
hidden-london

Swerve the actual Tube station and head 11 storeys underground. You can delve this deep only as part of tours run by the London Transport Museum – they run regularly but are popular and often sell out. The tour will take you to the station's deep-level shelter, around a mile of tunnels that were used by thousands of Londoners as bomb shelters during the Blitz and later as temporary accommodation for Windrush migrants in the late 1940s. The cramped space is frozen in time, with bunk beds and original signage all still there.

125 DOWN STREET STATION

Down St
W1J 7JU
Mayfair ⑥
+44 (0)343 222 5000
ltmuseum.co.uk/
hidden-london

London is dotted with old abandoned Tube stations that, for one reason or another, are no longer in use – you can spot what remains of Aldwych station on the Strand, for example. One of them, Down Street station, part of the Piccadilly Line between 1907 and 1932, is especially intriguing. After its closure Down Street went on to be covert wartime offices used by the Railway Executive Committee and frequented by Winston Churchill, who kipped overnight there, using the space as a secret bomb shelter. The tunnels, stairways and platforms were converted into offices and living quarters for staff, who lived and slept underground in shifts. On a Hidden London tour, you can spot the remnants – signage from this time, a telephone exchange, and rooms that, astonishingly, were wallpapered for the executives – as Piccadilly Line trains continue to rattle past.

BRUTALIST
beauties

_____

126 **BARBICAN**

Silk St
EC2Y 8DS
City of London ②
+44 (0)20 7638 4141
barbican.org.uk

A chunky, concrete icon – loved or hated by Londoners depending on their feelings about the stark style of brutalist architecture – the Barbican is both a world-class arts centre and a housing estate. Construction started in the 1960s on the terrace and high-rise tower blocks, built around ponds and green spaces, in an area that had been badly bombed during World War II. The Barbican Centre followed later in the 1980s. Nowadays you can visit the Grade II-listed stunner to catch a Royal Shakespeare Company play or a concert, watch a movie or be inspired at an art exhibition. Don't miss the Barbican Conservatory, a huge glass-roofed and somewhat surreal space filled with trailing greenery, exotic plants and fish.

127 **NATIONAL THEATRE**

Upper Ground
SE1 9PX
South Bank ③
+44 (0)20 7452 3000
nationaltheatre.org.uk

Brutalist architecture dominates the South Bank, thanks to the Southbank Centre and its neighbour the National Theatre. The bold building has divided public opinion since it opened in 1976, but there's no question it's one of the best theatres in the world. Make sure you eye the striking concrete waffle ceiling on your way to watch something brilliant in the Olivier auditorium.

128 SOUTHBANK CENTRE

Belvedere Road
SE1 8XX
South Bank ②
+44 (0)20 3879 9555
southbankcentre.co.uk

Not sure what you feel like doing? Head to the Southbank Centre. The geometric arts centre is the UK's biggest, made up of brutalist icon the Royal Festival Hall, contemporary art space the Hayward Gallery and events space Queen Elizabeth Hall – and it can fulfill any arty need. Built in 1951 as part of the Festival of Britain, it remains a beloved cultural hotspot. You can find free concerts, spoken-word performances, talks, exhibitions and huge festivals, like Meltdown, Women of the World and the London Literature Festival, within its concrete walls. It's also a prime strolling spot, thanks to its buzzy Thames-side location, great food and book markets, and outdoor spaces, like the Queen Elizabeth Hall Roof Gardens.

20TH-CENTURY
homes

129 **TRELLICK TOWER**

5 Golborne Road
W10 5PA
West ⑬

The skyline silhouette of Trellick Tower – a high-rise residential block flanked by a freestanding service tower – is visible from much of West London. Its 31 storeys, complete with 317 dwellings, were built between 1968 and 1975 as social housing to replace hundreds of homes in the area that were deemed unfit for habitation. The pillar of concrete and glass was considered to be the ultimate in modern living. It's still mainly social housing, with some pricey private residences. To snoop around inside, you can usually book onto tours during the annual Open House London architecture festival.

130 **2 WILLOW ROAD**

NW3 1TH
North ⑭
+44 (0)34 4800 1895
nationaltrust.org.
uk/2willowroad

Ernö Goldfinger, the architect who designed brutalist icon Trellick Tower, built this modernist masterpiece in 1939 as his family home. The design, featuring huge windows, a spiral staircase and an uncluttered interior, was considered to be groundbreaking at the time, even controversial. Much of the furniture inside the house was also designed by Goldfinger, while there's an impressive collection of modern art to look out for on the walls. The building is open to the public Wednesday to Sunday for most of the year.

131 ISOKON BUILDING

Lawn Road
NW3 2XD
North ⑭
+44 (0)77 1350 7018
isokongallery.co.uk

Sleek and space age, the Isokon Building was constructed in the 1930s as a sort of experiment in urban, minimalist living. This kind of reinforced concrete hadn't been used for residential purposes before, and, at the time, the communal lifestyle the building supported was radical. The functional flats were small and housekeeping was provided while meals could be taken in the Isobar downstairs, so residents weren't burdened with domestic drudgery. Famous occupants included author Agatha Christie and architect and founder of the Bauhaus School Walter Gropius. Open at the weekends only, the Isokon Gallery now exists on the ground floor to tell the building's story.

132 ALEXANDRA AND AINSWORTH ESTATE

Rowley Way
NW8 0SN
North ⑭

Constructed in the 1970s, this now-iconic, modernist housing estate was designed by architect Neave Brown, who worked for Camden Council at the time. The unique terraced design, which features a public park, school and community centre, is made up of low-rise flats built in a staggered style, so each has its own private outdoor space. The social housing is now a popular filming location, and it's easy to see why.

ART DECO
delights

---

133 HORNSEY TOWN HALL

The Broadway
N8 9JJ
North ⑭
hthartscentre.com

You've probably seen Hornsey Town Hall without realising it – the art deco icon has appeared in countless films and TV shows, from *Killing Eve* to *The Crown*, thanks to its unique 1930s interiors. Built as council offices, the HTH, with its dominating tower and long windows, became a cafe, arts centre and events space for the local community after administrative headquarters moved in the 1960s. A current regeneration project aims to preserve the creative essence of the building, conserve the public space's period features and turn some of the building into housing.

134 BROADCASTING HOUSE

Portland Place
W1A 1AA
Marylebone ⑥
+44 (0)20 8743 8000
bbc.co.uk

The curved and oddly asymmetrical home of the British Broadcasting Corporation was completed in 1932 as the BBC's first purpose-built building for radio broadcasting. Characterised by neat windows and a bold art deco clock tower, the building can be found just off Oxford Street. It's now two buildings, linked by a glass extension, and it is the place where much of the channel's radio shows and topical TV shows are recorded. You can't go inside but there are sometimes events or art installations in the building's courtyard.

135 ELTHAM PALACE

Court Yard
SE9 5QE
South ⑫
+44 (0)370 333 1181
english-heritage.org.uk/
eltham

Half art deco mansion, half medieval palace, Eltham Palace is an utterly enchanting place to discover. Once an important royal palace, moated Eltham was a favourite with a number of monarchs. It was presented to King Edward II in 1305 and the great hall that stands today was built for Edward IV in the 1470s, while Henry VIII is known to have spent much of his childhood there. After centuries of neglect, millionaires Stephen and Virginia Courtauld took the site, building a modern home that incorporated the ancient hall in 1933. Inside, it's eclectic and eccentric. Look out for the gloriously art deco dining room, Virginia's mosaic bathroom, complete with golden taps, and the centrally-heated enclosure their pet lemur Mah-Jongg enjoyed.

137 DENNIS SEVERS' HOUSE

Buildings
PRESERVED IN TIME

136 18 STAFFORD TERRACE

18 Stafford Terrace
W8 7BH
Kensington ④
+44 (0)20 7602 3316
rbkc.gov.uk/museums

The former residence of Punch cartoonist Edward Linley Sambourne, 18 Stafford Terrace is an incredible snapshot of a late-Victorian, middle-class home decked out in 'aesthetic interior' style. The Sambournes decorated their new home in the 1870s, and when it passed down through their family it remained largely as it was when they were alive, complete with original William Morris wallpaper, Japanese art, stained glass and the fashionable furniture of the time. It's now open to the public as a museum.

137 DENNIS SEVERS' HOUSE

18 Folgate St
E1 6BX
Spitalfields ⑨
+44 (0)20 7247 4013
dennissevers house.co.uk

There's a whole lot of life inside this old 17th-century terraced house, which was turned into an atmospheric journey through time by artist Dennis Severs. Once you've booked a slot to explore, you step through the front door and everything inside is designed to make you feel as though time is misbehaving. Each intensely decorated room of the four-floored home captures a moment in time for generations of a family of Huguenot silk weavers, from 1724 to 1914. You move through the scenes in silence while smells and sounds toy with your senses: ancient church bells appear to be ringing outside, there's a man's voice just out of earshot, a half-drunk cup of tea sits in front of you. Catch sight of yourself in one of the many mirrors and the sense that you've stepped into a painting is palpable. "You are here - ish" reads a piece of paper in one of the rooms and it couldn't feel more true.

138 EMERY WALKER'S HOUSE

7 Hammersmith
Terrace
W6 9TS
West ⑬
+44 (0)20 8741 4104
emerywalker.org.uk

A tall house at 7 Hammersmith Terrace, with a garden that runs down towards the Thames, was home to engraver and printer, and pal of William Morris, Emery Walker until 1933. Conserved exactly as it was when he was alive, the home is now considered to have the most complete and authentic arts and crafts interior in the UK. You'll find original, hand-blocked Morris & Co wallpapers in most rooms, as well as Philip Webb furniture and eclectic rugs and ceramics. See for yourself by booking on to a guided tour.

139 CARLYLE'S HOUSE

24 Cheyne Row
SW3 5HL
Chelsea ④
+44 (0)20 7352 7087
nationaltrust.org.uk/
carlyleshouse

Influential Victorian literary couple Thomas and Jane Carlyle called this Chelsea terraced house home from 1834 until their deaths. Carlyle was the instigator of The London Library, and the pair welcomed the likes of Charles Dickens, George Eliot and William Thackeray in through their front door. The home, which is still full of their personal possessions, was opened to the public shortly after Thomas died in 1881 and you can now wander around the time capsule it's become.

GRAND HOUSES
you can step inside

---

140 STRAWBERRY HILL HOUSE

268 Waldegrave
Road
TW1 4ST
West ⑬
+44 (0)20 8744 1241
*strawberryhillhouse.
org.uk*

A bright white masterpiece topped with decorative chimneys, turrets and battlements, Strawberry Hill House is the finest example of Georgian Gothic Revival architecture in Britain. The fascinating building came into being after writer and politician Horace Walpole purchased a couple of Thames-side cottages in 1747 and set about bringing his vision to life. The little Gothic castle became something of an attraction during his lifetime and continues to be today. The house, which inside has been restored to look as it would have done in the 1790s, and its grounds are open to the public.

141 HAM HOUSE

Ham St
TW10 7RS
West ⑬
+44 (0)20 8940 1950
*nationaltrust.org.uk/
hamhouse*

Set just back from the River Thames, Stuart stunner Ham House is a rare and extraordinary example of life during the 17th century. Built in 1610, it was turned into a grand home by royal courtier William Murray and later his daughter Elizabeth, Duchess of Lauderdale. Incredibly, it's changed so little in the centuries since Elizabeth's death that the house is pretty much exactly as she designed it today. Visit to slip through the family's richly decorated living quarters, filled with 400-year-old paintings and furniture, poke around below stairs in the kitchens and wander the ancient formal and kitchen gardens.

142 KENWOOD HOUSE

Hampstead Lane
NW3 7JR
North ⑭
+44 (0)37 0333 1181
english-heritage.org.
uk/kenwood

Perched on a grassy hill at the very top of Hampstead Heath, Kenwood House dates back to the early 17th century. You can wander through the ornate white villa's grand rooms, eyeing glittering chandeliers and bold paintwork or spotting Rembrandts. Don't miss the Great Library. Added in the 1760s, the room is lined with mirrors and old books and topped with a stunning pink and blue ceiling. Kenwood was the home of Dido Belle, a mixed-race woman who lived as part of an aristocratic family at the height of the slave trade. Her great-uncle Lord Chief Justice Mansfield, the most powerful judge in England at the time, was involved in the move towards the abolition of slavery. Her story was dramatised in the 2013 film *Belle*.

143 APSLEY HOUSE

149 Piccadilly
W1J 7NT
Mayfair ⑥
+44 (0)20 7499 5676
wellington
collection.co.uk

This grand townhouse once boasted the address 'Number 1 London' (it's now the slightly less impressive 149 Piccadilly). Built in the 1770s, it's the former London home of the first Duke of Wellington, who commanded the army that defeated Napoleon at the Battle of Waterloo. It's changed very little since the early 1800s, and the ornate interiors, featuring artworks and gifts from the Duke's influential friends, are gloriously over the top. Look out for gilded portraits, gleaming porcelain, bold yellow accents and the drawing room, which is kitted out in red and cream silk stripes. It's open to visitors.

144 CHARLTON HOUSE

Charlton Road
SE7 8RE
South ⑫
+44 (0)20 8856 3951
greenwichheritage.org/
charlton-house

When it was built in 1607 for the tutor of King James I's eldest son, this imposing red-brick and white stone manor house was in a rural hamlet, miles away from London's city walls. It's one of the finest Jacobean houses in the country, though alterations have been made over the centuries. The Chapel wing was rebuilt after being bombed in the Blitz, while the house is now also home to the Charlton Library. The house and the gardens are open for visitors.

Long-standing
ROYAL PALACES

145 BUCKINGHAM PALACE

SW1A 1AA
St James's ⑤
+44 (0)303 123 7300
rct.uk/buckingham palace

There's something very surreal about stepping inside Buckingham Palace, which members of the public are allowed to do for 10 weeks each year. The iconic London landmark is a working palace and the Queen's official residence, but ticket-holders are free to nosey around while she's on her summer holidays. Only a handful of rooms are open, but you can expect to see a lot of oil paintings, gilded ceilings, enormous chandeliers and loads of historic treasures, like Queen Victoria's 1837 throne. There's been a building on this site since the 17th century, but it became royal property in the 18th century and began to look like the grand palace it is today during the reign of Queen Vic.

146 HAMPTON COURT PALACE

KT8 9AU
East Molesey
+44 (0)33 3166 6000
hrp.org.uk/ hamptoncourtpalace

The former home of King Henry VIII and his myriad wives, Hampton Court Palace is a stunning Tudor palace beside the Thames in West London. The royal residence, which Queen Victoria opened to the public in 1838, is surrounded by huge ornamental gardens and the UK's oldest surviving hedge maze. The palace itself has been added to and redesigned over the years, as regal tastes have changed. Spy the king's private toilet, snoop around inside the ancient kitchens and imagine the extravagances of court life. Oh, and stay alert. Rumour has it the palace is haunted by a number of ghosts, including a couple of Henry's unlucky brides.

147 KENSINGTON PALACE

Kensington Gardens
W8 4PX
Kensington ④
+44 (0)33 3166 6000
hrp.org.uk/
kensingtonpalace

Despite the fact that this 17th-century palace is the actual home of The Duke and Duchess of Cambridge, Princess Charlotte and Princes George and Louis, as well as a handful of other royals, pretty Kensington Palace is open to the public seven days a week. You're unlikely to bump into Will and Kate, but you can look around grandly decorated rooms used by other royals, from William III and Mary II to a young Queen Victoria and Princess Diana.

148 SOMERSET HOUSE

Strand
WC2R 1LA
Covent Garden ①
+44 (0)20 7845 4600
somersethouse.org.uk

Before she was crowned Queen, Elizabeth I lived in a grand palace on this exact spot in central London. The last royal to live here left in 1693, and the building was rebuilt in the 1770s, when it then housed the Royal Academy of Arts, the Stamp Office and the General Register Office – but the grand neoclassical structure still makes for a royally good day out. Book onto a historical tour, or visit the arts centre for thought-provoking exhibitions, performances and events. During the summer, the courtyard plays host to film screenings and gigs, while in the winter it's transformed by a super-popular festive ice rink.

Impressive
TUDOR BUILDINGS

149 MIDDLE TEMPLE HALL

Middle Temple Lane
EC4Y 9AT
Holborn ①
+44 (0)20 7427 4820
*middletemple
venue.org.uk*

Middle Temple is one of the four Inns of Court – historic professional associations for the country's barristers that have existed since the 14th century. At its heart lies Middle Temple Hall, a perfectly preserved hall built in 1562 with an impressive hammerbeam roof. Though still in constant use, it's little changed since Tudor times. The high table is thought to have been a gift from Queen Elizabeth I, while the 'cupboard', a table used in ceremonies, is rumoured to be the hatch cover from the famous *Golden Hinde* ship. You can explore the hall, where William Shakespeare's *Twelfth Night* first played in 1602, on a pre-booked guided tour.

150 STAPLE INN

High Holborn
WC1V 7QJ
Holborn ①

Spotting Staple Inn as you pass down busy High Holborn feels like slipping back in time. The terraced Tudor buildings have been standing strong since 1586, while London has grown and changed around it. The slightly wonky structure really stands out on the street, which is populated with modern cafes and high-street shops. They've been modified over the years but remain a unique and eye-catching example of 16th-century timber-framed buildings.

HIGH
HOLBORN WC1

150 STAPLE INN

151 QUEEN ELIZABETH'S HUNTING LODGE

6 Rangers Road
E4 7QH
Chingford
+44 (0)20 7332 1911
cityoflondon.gov.uk

An extraordinary timber-framed building on the edge of Epping Forest, this hunting lodge was built in 1543 on the orders of Henry VIII, and may later have been used by his daughter when she hunted in the forest, too. You can explore the three floors, which are free to enter and open from Tuesday to Sunday, to dress up in Tudor-style costumes or enjoy views of the former royal hunting ground through the upstairs windows.

152 FULHAM PALACE

Bishop's Avenue
SW6 6EA
West ⑬
+44 (0)20 7736 3233
fulhampalace.org

Home to bishops from 704 until the 1970s, Fulham Palace (free and open daily) is a jigsaw of different architectural styles and fashions. The courtyard and great hall are Tudor, constructed around 1495. The courtyard, with its grand gatehouse and decorative brickwork, is especially evocative. You can almost see Queen Elizabeth I and her closest courtiers arriving for the feast in her honour in 1601.

153 SUTTON HOUSE

2 and 4 Homerton
High St
E9 6JQ
Hackney ⑩
+44 (0)20 8986 2264
nationaltrust.org.uk/
suttonhouse

Explore this atmospheric and remarkably intact Tudor house, which was built in the 1530s as the family home of Ralph Sadleir, a courtier of Henry VIII, self-guided at the weekends or on a bookable guided tour from Wednesday to Friday. The oldest home in Hackney has been modified over the years, and used for a variety of purposes. It was a Victorian school, a Trades Union office, and was even occupied by squatters in the 1980s, who left artwork on the building's walls. Even still, the sense of its Tudor heritage is palpable as soon as you see the original windows and carved fireplaces in Sutton House's moody, oak panelled rooms.

The OLDEST BUILDINGS
in London

---

154 52-55 NEWINGTON GREEN

N16 9PX

North ⑭

You could easily walk right by these townhouses on the west side of Newington Green without noticing them, but they're actually the oldest terraced houses in the city. Built in 1658, before the Great Fire of 1666, they are incredibly rare examples of 17th-century London homes.

155 41-42 CLOTH FAIR

EC1A 7JQ

City of London ②

Built in 1614, this corner construction with timber bay windows and a great arched entrance is the oldest inhabited house in the City of London – and the only one to survive the Great Fire of London. These days it's a private residence, where modern amenities sit alongside original details.

156 GUILDHALL

Basinghall St

EC2V 7HH

City of London ②

+44 (0)20 7332 1313

guildhall. cityoflondon.gov.uk

This grand building has been the administrative and ceremonial centre of the City of London since the Middle Ages, being built between 1411 and 1440. It's been the setting for trials – like that of 17-year-old Lady Jane Grey, who was queen for nine days between Edward VI and Mary I before being convicted of high treason – as well as pageants and parties. The Great Hall's roof was destroyed during a WWII air raid and replaced in 1953 but many ancient, original features remain. Book onto a monthly tour to see inside the building.

157 TOWER OF LONDON

EC3N 4AB
City of London ②
+44 (0)33 3320 6000
hrp.org.uk/tower-of-london

No surprises, the Tower of London is old. It's where Anne Boleyn was famously held before her execution, where Guy Fawkes was interrogated and where two young princes vanished in 1483. But the oldest part is The White Tower. Built in 1078 by William the Conqueror, it's actually the oldest intact building in all of London. The rest of the world-famous castle grew around it and on a visit there today you can also see features from the 13th and 16th centuries, as well as the iconic Beefeaters, the Tower's loyal ravens and the Crown Jewels. Book onto a Twilight Tour or to see The Ceremony of the Keys for an extra atmospheric experience.

158 THE CHARTERHOUSE

Charterhouse Square
EC1M 6AN
City of London ②
+44 (0)20 7253 9503
thecharterhouse.org

Built in 1371 on the site of a plague pit, the Charterhouse was originally a Catholic priory. It transformed into a Tudor manor house after the dissolution of the monasteries – Elizabeth I is known to have met the Privy Council here before her 1558 coronation – while, in the early 17th century, the purpose of the Charterhouse changed again, becoming a boys' school and almshouses for the elderly and in need. It still houses over 40 'brothers' (women have lived here since 2018 but the name endures) in unique and peaceful surroundings today. See all that history up-close by booking a tour.

159 THE PALACE OF WESTMINSTER

SW1A 0AA
Westminster ⑤
parliament.uk

Both the living heart of modern politics and a piece of ancient history, the Palace of Westminster is a fascinating place. The home of UK Parliament, it's where bills and laws are debated in incredible surroundings. Much of it dates from 1834, when the Palace was rebuilt following a huge fire. Westminster Hall, though, is older. Built in 1097 with an impressive timber roof, which was added in the 14th century, it's pretty much the only part of the ancient Palace of Westminster still standing. Tours of the Palace take place on Saturdays and some weekdays when Parliament is not in session. The tiny Jewel Tower nearby, which was built in 1365, is another survivor from the original Palace and is open to visitors daily.

LEIGHTON HOUSE MUSEUM

ART & CULTURE

Grand
MUSEUMS

———————

160 **V&A**
Cromwell Road
SW7 2RL
Kensington ④
+44 (0)20 7942 2000
vam.ac.uk

A cathedral of creativity, the V&A is one of the very best museums in the world. Inside, you'll find a celebration of the decorative arts with permanent exhibition spaces dedicated to fine jewellery, beautiful ceramics, intricate glassware, sculpture, textiles and fashion, spanning 5000 years of artistic history, all for free. The buildings themselves are reason enough to visit. Queen Victoria laid the foundation stone in May 1899 for a space intended to showcase the best of contemporary design. It's been developed over the decades but the V&A, with its decorative domes and arches, remains an extraordinary example of Victorian architecture.

161 **NATURAL HISTORY MUSEUM**
Cromwell Road
SW7 5BD
Kensington ④
+44 (0)20 7942 5000
nhm.ac.uk

The Natural History Museum and its stunning, cavernous terracotta building opened in 1881 to house the British Museum's growing collection of artefacts and specimens. At the time, new species and plants were being discovered regularly and it was designed to be big enough to showcase huge items like dinosaur skeletons. The space contains an extraordinary number of historical exhibits, while continuing important research that shines a light on our current struggles. Just as it was when it opened, the NHM is free to enter.

162 BRITISH MUSEUM

Great Russell St
WC1B 3DG
Bloomsbury ⑦
+44 (0)20 7323 8000
britishmuseum.org

Founded in 1753 after Sir Hans Soane left his collection of more than 70.000 objects to the nation, the British Museum became the first national public museum in the world. It was free to 'all curious persons' and continues to be so today. Visit to see fascinating objects like cat mummies, letters written by Roman soldiers and a 1,8 million-year-old stone tool, as well as world-famous artefacts like the Rosetta Stone.

Old-school
HALLS

163 WILTON'S MUSIC HALL

1 Graces Alley
E1 8JB
East ⑪
+44 (0)20 7702 2789
wiltons.org.uk

You'll forget all about 21st-century London during a visit to Wilton's Music Hall. A charming Victorian concert hall, Wilton's ran in atmospheric Graces Alley between 1859 and 1881. It's miraculously managed to survive pretty much intact, despite the fact that it was used as a soup kitchen and a rag-sorting warehouse in the intervening years. After a sensitive refurb, Wilton's is back doing what it does best: putting on cabaret, theatre and musical performances. The peeling paint, exposed brickwork and crumbly vibes just add to the building's utter charm.

164 RIVOLI BALLROOM

350 Brockley Road
SE4 2BY
South ⑫
+44 (0)20 8692 5130
rivoliballroom.com

A retro ballroom complete with Chinese lanterns and rich red and gold interiors, the Rivoli is astonishingly well preserved. It's famous for its 1950s styling but the space actually first opened in 1913, and has been welcoming foxtrot fans and charleston champs ever since. You can still drop by to boogie at a Jive Party, or, if sitting down is more your thing, attempt to keep your eyes on the action (and not the sparkling chandeliers) at a movie screening.

165 TROXY

490 Commercial
Road
E1 0HX
East ⑪
+44 (0)20 7790 9000
troxy.co.uk

If good things come in small packages, Troxy is the exception to the rule. This beast of an art deco cinema opened in 1933 as the biggest cinema in England with capacity for 3520 film lovers. The reels stopped turning in the 1960s and after a stint as the Royal Opera Centre and a stretch as a bingo hall, Troxy is now an events space, hosting concerts, gigs, immersive performances and festivals.

166 BUSH HALL

310 Uxbridge Road
W12 7LJ
West ⑬
+44 (0)20 8222 6955
bushhallmusic.co.uk

Built in 1904, Bush Hall was one of a trio of halls a father commissioned for his three daughters (talk about a good present). Over the last century it's been a snooker hall, a soup kitchen and The Who's rehearsal space. Now it's a live music venue that, thanks to its glittering light-fittings and delicate cornicing, manages to retain its early-20th-century glamour, no matter who is on the stage.

Historic
CINEMAS

---

167 THE SCREEN ON THE GREEN

83 Upper St
N1 0NP
Islington ⑧
+44 (0)87 2436 9060
*everymancinema.com/
screen-on-the-green*

The Screen on the Green's red neon signage is an iconic London sight. The cinema has been open for more than 100 years. It's changed hands a few times over the decades, but the quirky little building, surrounded by bars, cafes and swanky shops, has continued to welcome film fans since 1913, making it one of the oldest continuously running cinemas in the UK. Inside, it's all plush sofa seats and fancy service, but it has some serious street cred, too. The cinema played host to live performances from The Clash and The Sex Pistols in the 1970s.

167 THE SCREEN ON THE GREEN

168 ELECTRIC CINEMA

191 Portobello Road
W11 2ED
West ⑬
+44 (0)20 7908 9696
electriccinema.co.uk

Cinemagoers can snuggle up on velvet double beds under cashmere blankets to watch a blockbuster at the Electric. The cinema has been screening films to Londoners since 1911, but it wasn't always as luxurious inside. There were a few grubby, run-down decades, when it was officially called The Imperial and affectionately nicknamed 'the fleapit'. It became the Electric in the 1970s, and gained a reputation for screening rare and daring movies that you couldn't see anywhere else in the city. These days the Grade II-listed beauty is run by Soho House and, while the original proscenium arch still surrounds the screen, there isn't a flea in sight.

169 THE CASTLE CINEMA

64-66 Brooksby's
Walk
E9 6DA
Hackney ⑲
thecastlecinema.com

This cute community cinema in Clapton has had a varied past. Since opening in 1913 as a single-screen cinema, it's been a bingo hall, a shoe factory and a snooker club. The Castle returned to its filmic roots in 2017 thanks to a local couple who painstakingly restored it and the Londoners who funded the renovation on Kickstarter. Visit to spot original features, like the beautiful curved ceiling and gold, ornate plasterwork, and relax at the bar, which channels the cinema's long history with art deco interiors.

170 RIO CINEMA

107 Kingsland
High St
E8 2PB
Hackney ⑲
+44 (0)20 7241 9410
riocinema.org.uk

One of London's very first cinemas opened on this spot in 1909 but the eye-catching art deco building that you can find today is straight out of the 1930s. The retro lettering, lit-up façade and bold, technicolour interior looks much the same today as it did when cult architect F.E. Bromige designed it. You can't see it as you munch your popcorn, but above the cinema's mauve ceiling lies the remains of the original, domed auditorium too.

171 EVERYMAN MUSWELL HILL

Fortis Green Road
N10 3HP
North ⑭
+44 (0)87 2436 9060
everymancinema.com/
muswell-hill

Muswell Hill's Grade II-listed Everyman cinema first opened in 1936 and visiting today you'd never guess a day had gone by. One of 78 art deco cinemas in Britain designed by architect George Coles, the building recently underwent a renovation to restore it to its original and totally beautiful state. Stepping inside the stunning art deco foyer is like travelling back in time.

172 PHOENIX CINEMA

52 High Road
N2 9PJ
North ⑭
+44 (0)20 8444 6789
phoenixcinema.co.uk

It might not be much of a looker from the outside, but the much-loved Phoenix – a not-for-profit cinema operated by a charitable trust on behalf of North Londoners – really is special. Inside, it's an art deco, single-screen beauty with vaulted ceilings and unusual design flourishes. This vibrant aesthetic has been greeting cinemagoers for more than 100 years, when the East Finchley Picturedrome first opened.

MUSEUMS *that*
USED TO BE HOMES

---

173 SIR JOHN SOANE'S MUSEUM

13 Lincoln's Inn Fields
WC2A 3BP
Holborn ①
+44 (0)20 7405 2107
soane.org

The former house of celebrated 19th-century architect Sir John Soane is both a beautifully curated museum and a fascinating time capsule. At his request, the building has barely been touched since his death more than 180 years ago. Now, when you visit you can tour Soane's private apartments as well as rooms packed full of assorted treasures he collected during his lifetime, such as statues, great art, furniture and 3000-year-old Egyptian sarcophagi. The house is open Wednesday to Sunday and it's free to enter but you have to book in advance.

174 KEATS HOUSE

10 Keats Grove
NW3 2RR
North ⑭
+44 (0)20 7332 3868
cityoflondon.gov.uk

This white Georgian villa in leafy Hampstead is so pretty it'll make you want to start writing poetry. It's what writer John Keats did when he lived here between 1818 and 1820, in what was then a rural, creative neighbourhood. Open to visitors from Wednesday to Sunday, the house is home to changing exhibitions as well as talks, walks and workshops.

175 DOWN HOUSE

Luxted Road
BR6 7JT
Orpington
+44 (0)16 8985 9119
english-heritage. org.uk/downhouse

As the former home of world-famous scientist Charles Darwin, Down House has witnessed its share of incredible feats. You can stand in the study where Darwin penned *On the Origin of Species* or explore the abundant gardens where he conducted many of his experiments. Hunt out the nondescript-looking worm stone, which Darwin used to measure soil movement as it was displaced by worms under the ground.

176 HANDEL & HENDRIX IN LONDON

25 Brook St
W1K 4HB
Mayfair ⑥
+44 (0)20 7495 1685
handelhendrix.org

By some incredible chance, these two totally different musical masters lived in roughly the same spot, two centuries apart. Their homes, at 23 and 25 Brook Street, are now connected as part of this small but fascinating museum. The ancient and incredibly creaky floorboards of classical composer George Frideric Handel's former house, where he lived from 1723 until his death, will transport you back to another time, before you climb up to the small flat Jimi Hendrix and his girlfriend Kathy Etchingham rented in the late 1960s. Spot half-smoked cigarettes, groovy wall hangings and bottles of Mateus Rosé in the cleverly reconstructed bedroom. In the second room, a window opens out onto a flat roof, where you'll swear you can almost see Hendrix climbing out for a smoke.

176 HANDEL & HENDRIX IN LONDON

177 CHARLES DICKENS MUSEUM

48 Doughty St
WC1N 2LX
Bloomsbury ⑦
+44 (0)20 7405 2127
dickensmuseum.com

Author Charles Dickens wrote *Oliver Twist*, *The Pickwick Papers* and *Nicholas Nickleby* when he was living in this neat Georgian terrace with his young family. You can explore the family's bedrooms, the servants' quarters, the dining room (all laid out for a meal) and Dickens's study, filled with handwritten letters and original manuscripts. Visit when the museum stays open into the evening for an extra-atmospheric experience.

178 WILLIAM MORRIS GALLERY

AT: LLOYD PARK
Forest Road
E17 4PP
Walthamstow ⑪
+44 (0)20 8496 4390
wmgallery.org.uk

Writer, socialist and creator of incredible wallpaper William Morris lived in this grand Walthamstow house as a young man. Built in the 1740s, it was Morris's family home between 1848 and 1856. You can expect to find rugs, tiles, fabrics and elaborate prints, as well as personal items belonging to Morris, on a visit there today. The Gallery is free to visit Tuesday to Sunday. Love arts and crafts? Visit the William Morris Society's museum in the coach house of Kelmscott House, where he lived from 1878 until his death in 1896, and Red House, a stunning home commissioned by the artist, which is also open to the public.

179 LEIGHTON HOUSE MUSEUM

12 Holland Park
Road
W14 8LZ
Kensington ④
+44 (0)20 7602 3316
rbkc.gov.uk/museums

This must be one of the most stunning houses on the planet. The former home and studio of successful Victorian artist Lord Frederic Leighton, it was built and decorated to his design from the 1860s onwards. Behind its plain exterior, Leighton House is filled with sumptuous and ambitious interiors, featuring art and items from his travels. The rooms are richly decorated with tiles, marble pillars and silk wallpaper. Pause in the Arab room, a later addition to Leighton's home, glittering with gold mosaic and beautiful tiles from the late 15th and early 16th centuries. The house is open for visits, as well as for regular creative workshops, talks and concerts.

London's oldest
THEATRES

180 THEATRE ROYAL DRURY LANE

Catherine St
WC2B 5JF
Covent Garden ①
+44 (0)20 7557 7300
lwtheatres.co.uk/
theatres/theatre-royal-
drury-lane

The world's oldest theatre site in continuous use – this is known to have been a spot for entertainment since 1663 – Theatre Royal Drury Lane is as theatrical as the productions that are put on here. The current building, complete with two ornate royal boxes, first welcomed theatregoers in 1812. An ongoing restoration plans to return the theatre to how it looked in the early 19th century, when it was rebuilt after a fire, but with improved accessibility, an all-day restaurant and roomier seating. An original staircase from 1812 will also be returned to pride of place.

181 THEATRE ROYAL HAYMARKET

18 Suffolk St
SW1Y 4HT
Piccadilly ⑤
+44 (0)20 7930 8800
trh.co.uk

A much-loved part of London's theatre scene since 1720, Theatre Royal Haymarket can count Queen Victoria, Queen Elizabeth II and Oscar Wilde among its former patrons – and Noel Coward, Vivian Leigh and Maggie Smith among the stars who have trod its boards. Rebuilt in 1820, the playhouse and its opulently decorated auditorium is now a protected, Grade I-listed part of the West End.

182 ADELPHI THEATRE

Strand
WC2R 0NS
Covent Garden ①
+44 (0)20 7087 7753
lwtheatres.co.uk/
theatres/adelphi

It's changed names (and been rebuilt) more than a couple of times over the years, but there's been a theatre where the Adelphi now sits since 1806. The current building dates from the 1930s. It was designed by architect Ernest Schaufelberg and is peppered with art deco features. Make sure you admire the retro façade and 1930s signage on your way into the foyer.

183 ROYAL OPERA HOUSE

Bow St
WC2E 9DD
Covent Garden ①
+44 (0)20 7304 4000
roh.org.uk

You might lose track of the onstage action at the Royal Opera House, thanks to the auditorium's elegant horseshoe-shaped balconies, ornamental plasterwork and gilded decor. The building's beautiful, classical design has been virtually unchanged since it was rebuilt (for the third time) after a fire in the 1850s. Explore the stunning surroundings by booking tickets to a show, taking a backstage tour or popping by for a drink – the building is open to visitors every day from 10 am. It all feels like stepping out of 21st-century London and into another era entirely.

184 VAUDEVILLE THEATRE

404 Strand
WC2R 0NH
Covent Garden ①
+44 (0)33 0333 4814
nimaxtheatres.com/vaudeville-theatre

This stalwart of the West End, with its pretty glazed canopy, has been putting on shows since 1870. It's been redeveloped a couple of times since, but original features from each period remain, like the fan-shaped decorative ceiling in the auditorium, which has been there since the theatre first opened its doors. The building you find there today mainly dates back to 1926, when the Vaudeville was refurbished to include more seating and a sizeable, rectangle auditorium.

185 SAVOY THEATRE

Savoy Court
WC2R 0ET
Covent Garden ①
+44 (0)84 4871 7687
thesavoytheatre.com

Gleaming, glittering and really quite distracting when you're watching a performance here, the interior of the Savoy Theatre is something else. Originally opened in 1881, the theatre is famous for being the first public building in the world to be lit by electricity. 40 years later, the Victorian auditorium was replaced in art deco style. It was that theatrical, mirrored and metallic design from the 1920s that was then later faithfully restored after a fire in the 1990s. So unlike any other modern building, it's a totally immersive experience.

MUSEUMS *about* LONDON'S PAST

186 MUSEUM OF LONDON

150 London Wall
EC2Y 5HN
City of London ②
+44 (0)20 7001 9844
*museumof
london.org.uk*

A one-stop-shop for London's history, the Museum of London is a must-visit. Based near the Barbican and ancient sections of London Wall (though plans are currently in place to relocate the site to dilapidated market buildings in Smithfield), the museum is an authority on the past, present and future of the city. Explore permanent (and free) exhibitions about Roman Londinium right up to the London 2012 Olympic games, via plague, fire, war, social reform and urban expansion. The museum also hosts walks, talks and workshops. The Museum of London Docklands, a second site dedicated to telling the story of London's relationship with the river and the city's once thriving docks, is also well worth a visit.

187 BLACK CULTURAL ARCHIVES

1 Windrush Square
SW2 1EF
South ⑫
+44 (0)20 3757 8500
*blackcultural
archives.org*

The only national heritage centre dedicated to the histories of African and Caribbean people in Britain, the Black Cultural Archives is doing an invaluable job collecting and celebrating previously untold stories. Set in a Grade II-listed building in Brixton's Windrush Square, you'll find a space for research, reading, screenings and talks, as well as regular exhibitions that reflect Britain's rich, black history.

188 LONDON TRANSPORT MUSEUM

**Covent Garden
Piazza
WC2E 7BB
Covent Garden ①
+44 (0)34 3222 5000
*ltmuseum.co.uk***

Learn about how the city has changed over the last 200 years through the modes of transport Londoners have used to get around. This family-friendly museum is packed full of Victorian horse-drawn buses, early Tube carriages and train engines, as well as retro travel posters and the original, now iconic, Tube map. Keep an eye out for open days at LTM's Museum Depot in Acton, too. The store, which is home to more than 320.000 historical objects, opens to visitors a handful of times a year.

189 MUSEUM OF THE HOME

**136 Kingsland Road
E2 8EA
Hackney ⑩
+44 (0)20 7739 9893
*museumof
thehome.org.uk***

You'll find the Museum of the Home in a set of 18th-century almshouses. Concerned with the minutiae of domestic life, this museum paints a vivid picture of how people in the past ate, slept, washed and lived, through furniture, textiles, decorative art and practical objects. Parts of the almshouses have been turned into accurate yet evocative snapshots of life in the 18th and 19th centuries, and you can also wander through fascinating rooms based on real, middle-class London homes from 1630 to 1990.

Age-old
ART GALLERIES

190 ROYAL ACADEMY OF ARTS

AT: BURLINGTON HOUSE
Piccadilly
W1J 0BD
Mayfair ⑥
+44 (0)20 7300 8090
royalacademy.org.uk

The RA was founded in 1768 by a group of artists and architects as a society for promoting the arts. The gallery was initially based at Somerset House, and then shared space with the National Gallery, before moving to its current and historic home at Burlington House in 1867. Known for its world-class shows, the RA continues to put on an annual Summer Exhibition – the largest open-submission art show in the world – which has taken place every year since 1769. Don't miss the wooden prototype for Britain's now-iconic red phone boxes, which can be found in the gallery's arched entrance.

190 ROYAL ACADEMY OF ARTS

191 NATIONAL GALLERY

Trafalgar Square
WC2N 5DN
Covent Garden ①
+44 (0)20 7747 2885
nationalgallery.org.uk

A purpose-built home for the National Gallery first opened in 1838. Located in the heart of the city, it was always free to enter and open to everyone from all walks of life to come and learn about the great art hanging on its walls. Visit today to see art that spans centuries, from Van Gogh's *Sunflowers* to Leonardo da Vinci's *Virgin of the Rocks*. Don't leave without going next door to the National Portrait Gallery to look into the eyes of the likes of William Shakespeare, Elizabeth I, Henry VIII and Queen Victoria.

192 DULWICH PICTURE GALLERY

Gallery Road
SE21 7AD
South ⑫
+44 (0)20 8693 5254
dulwichpicture
gallery.org.uk

This modest building in South London is England's oldest public art gallery. Home to masterpieces by Rembrandt, Rubens, Constable and Gainsborough, Dulwich Picture Gallery was established in 1811, after painter Sir Francis Bourgeois and dealer Noel Desenfans bequeathed their impressive art collection to Dulwich College with the instruction that the works should be available for the public to view.

Curious
EXHIBITS

193 THE OLD OPERATING THEATRE MUSEUM

9a St Thomas St
SE1 9RY
South Bank ②
+44 (0)20 7188 2679
*oldoperating
theatre.com*

Museum exhibits don't get much more atmospheric – or grisly – than this. An astonishingly well-preserved operating theatre, the set-up was in use from 1822 until 1862, and is the oldest surviving surgical theatre in Europe. It's in the roof space above St Thomas' Church, with a light well to help surgeons see what they were doing and seating for more than 100 students to watch. This was a pre-anaesthesia and antiseptic era and, after you hear more about the gruesome things that went on here in the name of medicine, you'll be glad it only feels like you've gone back in time.

194 POLLOCK'S TOY MUSEUM

1 Scala St
W1T 2HL
Fitzrovia ⑦
+44 (0)20 7636 3452
pollockstoys.com

Two historic buildings in Fitzrovia are home to fascinating cabinets of old toys. From a 4000-year-old Egpytian clay mouse to 1970s puzzles, Victorian dolls and old-fashioned teddy bears, quirky Pollock's is teeming with childhood nostalgia. Make your way through the narrow passageways, past pre-loved toys, and you'll be reminiscing about your own former faves in no time.

195 MUSEUM OF BRANDS

111-117 Lancaster
Road
W11 1QT
West ⑬
+44 (0)20 7243 9611
museumofbrands.com

Who knew cereal boxes could be this fascinating? Visit the Museum of Brands to wander through their Time Tunnel, a space that charts the history of consumerism from the Victorian era to the modern day, via loads of gorgeous retro packaging. Toys, posters, magazine covers and adverts also line the walls as the exhibition takes you back in time through social changes like women's suffrage, feminism and the growth of plastic consumption.

196 HORNIMAN MUSEUM & GARDENS

100 London Road
SE23 3PQ
South ⑫
+44 (0)20 8699 1872
horniman.ac.uk

The Horniman has been welcoming curious visitors since Victorian times, when founder Frederick John Horniman first opened his house and put his personal collection of anthropological objects on display. There's an aquarium, a butterfly house, a music gallery and a small zoo but the real draw is the natural history gallery – presided over by an anatomically-incorrect, overstuffed walrus – where exhibits are displayed in traditional cases, just like they would have been over a century ago.

Nostalgic
NIGHTS OUT

197 THE MOUSETRAP
AT: ST MARTIN'S THEATRE
West St
WC2H 9NZ
Covent Garden ①
+44 (0)20 7836 1443
uk.the-mousetrap.co.uk

London's West End is no stranger to successful, long-running productions but nothing beats Agatha Christie's *The Mousetrap*. The tale, which is one of Christie's gripping murder mysteries, has been running continuously since 1952. It's been at its current location at St Martin's Theatre since 1974. Spot the sign in the foyer keeping track of the show's record-breaking number of performances.

198 RONNIE SCOTT'S
47 Frith St
W1D 4HT
Soho ①
+44 (0)20 7439 0747
ronniescotts.co.uk

A much-loved Soho institution, Ronnie Scott's has been entertaining music lovers since 1959. Opened by British saxophonist Ronnie Scott, the club was the first to welcome American jazz musicians in the UK and has gone on to host legendary performers such as Miles Davis. With its intimate vibe and late-night opening hours, it's now one of the most famous jazz clubs in the world.

199 TROUBADOUR
263-267 Old
Brompton Road
SW5 9JA
Chelsea ④
+44 (0)20 7341 6333
troubadourlondon.com

Opened as a Greenwich Village-style coffee house in 1954, the retro Troubadour has changed very little since then. It still serves coffee, as well as booze and comfort food, but the spot is probably better known for its live music performances. Bob Dylan (under a pseudonym), Paul Simon, Stones drummer Charlie Watts, Joni Mitchell and Jimi Hendrix have all played here over the years.

200 BUZZ BINGO TOOTING

50 Mitcham Road
SW17 9NA
South ⑫
+44 (0)20 8672 5717
buzzbingo.com/club/
tooting.html

The lavishly decorated interior of this huge bingo hall in Tooting, fitted out with Gothic arches and faux-medieval style friezes, is totally unexpected. You'll still find everything you need for an evening playing this traditional game – neat rows of tables and chairs, games machines, pots of dabbers – but you might struggle to keep your eyes on the prize. When the Grade I-listed space opened as a cinema in 1931 it must have been one of the most extraordinary cinemas in the world. It has to be seen to be believed.

201 SHAKESPEARE'S GLOBE

21 New Globe Walk
SE1 9DT
South Bank ③
+44 (0)20 7401 9919
shakespearesglobe.com

It might not have been standing since William Shakespeare's time – opened in the late 1990s, the Globe is a recreation of the playhouse Shakespeare wrote for, close to its original site – but that doesn't stop a night out here feeling compellingly authentic. Especially if you opt for a 'groundling' ticket (a bargain at 5 pound) and watch a live performance while standing up in the open-air yard, like the majority of Elizabethan theatregoers would have done. Shakespeare plays – often experimental and with star-studded casts – are performed in the timber-framed, thatched roof theatre during the summer months, while guided tours take place all year around.

202 ROWANS TENPIN BOWL

10 Stroud Green Road
N4 2DF
North ⑭
+44 (0)20 8800 1950
rowans.co.uk

You can bowl, boogie, sing, slurp slushies (and booze) and stay out late at Rowans in Finsbury Park. A former cinema, which – according to police complaints – was a rather raucous place during the 1910s, Rowans Bowl has barely changed in the last few decades. Visit to admire the faded decor and retro signs – and enjoy the buzzy, community atmosphere.

THE OLD CINEMA

3/-

SHOPS

Perfectly preserved
FOOD *and* DRINK SHOPS

203 PAXTON & WHITFIELD

93 Jermyn St
SW1Y 6JE
St James's ⑤
+44 (0)20 7930 0259
*paxtonand
whitfield.co.uk*

The smell of more than 100 delicious, artisanal cheeses hits
you as soon as you step inside Paxton & Whitfield. The shop on
Jermyn Street, with its vintage gold and black frontage, has been
trading since 1896, but its history goes back further to a man
called Stephen Cullum, who set up a cheese stall in Aldwych
market in 1742. As business grew, he took on two partners –
Harry Paxton and Charles Whitfield – whose names (and oddly
not his) are now forever associated with really good cheese.
Paxton & Whitfield gained its first Royal Warrant (a prestigious
mark of recognition given to companies who have regularly
supplied goods to a royal household) from Queen Victoria in
1850 and are cheesemongers to the current Queen today.

204 CHARBONNEL ET WALKER

AT: THE ROYAL ARCADE
28 Old Bond St
W1S 4BT
Mayfair ⑥
+44 (0)20 7318 2075
charbonnel.co.uk

One of Britain's first chocolatiers, Charbonnel et Walker still
stands on its original spot at the entrance to The Royal Arcade.
A joint venture for Mrs Walker and Madame Charbonnel, who
had learned her skills from the Maison Boissier chocolate
house in Paris, the shop first started selling sweet treats
in 1875. Chocolates are still handmade using Charbonnel's
traditional recipes, and are packaged in beautiful, vintage-
style boxes.

205 BERRY BROS. & RUDD

3 St James's St
SW1Y 5HZ
St James's ⑤
+44 (0)20 7022 8973
bbr.com

3 St James's Street has been the home of Berry Bros. & Rudd, the oldest wine and spirit merchants in Britain and the wine supplier of choice to the royal family, since 1698. The shop itself has been basically unchanged since the 18th century – its dark exterior, embellished with neat gold lettering and a fluttering flag, is something from a bygone era. Step inside and the historic delights continue. You'll find a giant pair of coffee scales, used to weigh coffee, tea... and the shop's customers. Records spanning three centuries detail the weights of the likes of Lord Byron and countless royals. Look out for a letter on the wall, too. Dated 15 April 1912, it's from the White Star Line informing Berry Bros of the loss of 69 cases of its wines and spirits in the sinking of the Titanic. To buy bottles of the good stuff, head around the corner to Berry Bros. & Rudd's newer store at 63 Pall Mall.

206 TWININGS

216 Strand
WC2R 1AP
Covent Garden ①
+44 (0)20 7353 3511
twinings.co.uk/
216-strand

Have you even visited London if you haven't visited the city's oldest tea shop? 216 Strand was purchased by cuppa-lover Thomas Twining in the early 1700s and the narrow little shop has been keeping the city's teapots pouring ever since. Follow in the footsteps of Jane Austen, who wrote about visiting the store in her diary, and visit to stock up on a traditional loose leaf blend.

207 ALGERIAN COFFEE STORES

52 Old Compton St
W1D 4PB
Soho ①
+44 (0)20 7437 2480
algerian
coffeestores.com

Caffeine fiends are in their element at Algerian Coffee Stores, which stocks coffee machines and accessories, as well as more than 80 coffee blends for that perfect pick-me-up. Tea drinkers are also catered for at the Soho stalwart, which has been trading from the same shop since 1887. Inside there's a buzzy, slightly chaotic vibe that might be fueled by the punchy 1 pound espressos being served, either to take away or to sip standing up.

208 LINA STORES

18 Brewer St
W1F 0SH
Soho ①
+44 (0)20 7437 6482
linastores.co.uk

If you're a sucker for all things Italian, you can't beat Lina Stores. The green-tiled delicatessen first opened in 1944 and it's still selling lush produce, fresh pasta, bread, antipasti and dreamy cannoli from the corner of Brewer Street and Green's Court. While you're in the area, head on to 51 Greek Street, just a few minutes away, to sample a dish of that handmade pasta with a glass of vino rosso at Lina Stores' tiny Soho restaurant.

209 W. MARTYN

135 Muswell Hill
Broadway
N10 3RS
North ⑭
+44 (0)20 8883 5642
wmartyn.co.uk

Established in 1897, this family-run speciality food shop in North London is proud of its old-fashioned feel – it's now run by the great-grandson of the original owner. The interior of the shop has hardly changed over the last century. You'll still find teas, coffees, biscuits, jams, chutneys and other fancy store-cupboard fare stacked up on the original Victorian shelves. Spot a beautiful, old set of scales on the counter and the coffee roaster in the window, which has been running daily since the 1950s.

SPECIALIST
shops

---

210 JAMES SMITH & SONS

53 New Oxford St
WC1A 1BL
Holborn ①
+44 (0)20 7836 4731
james-smith.co.uk

In this city you're going to need a brolly, and there's nowhere better than James Smith & Sons to get one. They've been selling umbrellas, walking sticks and parasols to Londoners since 1830, and from this very shop since 1857. Go to select a high-end handmade umbrella, but stay to marvel at the untouched interiors and gorgeous Victorian signage. Some of the original signs are from the other James Smith & Sons branches. There used to be six stores, but all the fixtures and fittings ended up here after they closed.

211 JAMES J. FOX

19 St James's St
SW1A 1ES
St James's ⑤
+44 (0)20 7930 3787
jjfox.co.uk

Cigars, tobacco and smoking accessories have been sold from 19 St James's Street since 1787, when Robert Lewis set up shop. The store's current name comes from James J. Fox, a brand formed in Dublin in 1881, who bought the business in the 1990s. The shop still sells the same traditional fare. There's also a museum in the shop's basement where you can find cigars and cigar cases owned by Churchill, a glass smoking pipe from the year the shop opened and the oldest box of Havana cigars in existence.

212 LOCK & CO.

6 St James's St
SW1A 1EF
St James's ⑤
+44 (0)20 7930 8874
lockhatters.co.uk

Lock & Co. is considered to be the oldest hat shop in the world. You've been able to buy fine and fancy hats on St James's Street since 1678 – and from this narrow little shop since 1765. Famous heads that have shopped here include Admiral Lord Nelson, Oscar Wilde, Charlie Chaplin, Sir Winston Churchill and Jackie Kennedy. Hats aren't as big of a deal as they used to be, but Lock & Co. continues to sell headwear from its historic spot today.

213 DAVENPORTS MAGIC SHOP

7 Charing Cross
Underground Arcade
WC2N 4HZ
Covent Garden ①
+44 (0)20 7836 0408
davenportsmagic.co.uk

Hidden away in the most unlikely of places, Davenports Magic Shop is the oldest continuously owned magic shop on the planet. Founded in 1898 by Lewis Davenport, the business has been in the same family ever since. It's moved around a bit and today can be found in a run-down underground arcade below the Strand – it's actually inside Charing Cross station – with not much else for company. But if you're after cards, must-have illusionist accessories, books or even a beginners' magic course, there's nowhere better.

214 FLORIS

89 Jermyn St
SW1Y 6JH
St James's ⑤
+44 (0)20 7930 2885
florislondon.com

This delightfully scented perfumery shop on Jermyn Street, with its gilded lettering, Union Jack flag and royal coat of arms, is pretty as a postcard. Floris, which is the only perfumer to hold a Royal Warrant from the Queen, has been in business since 1730 and is still run by descendants of Juan Famenias and Elizabeth Floris, who set up shop selling perfumes, combs, toothbrushes and shaving products all those years ago.

215 ASPREY

167 New Bond St
W1S 4AY
Mayfair ⑥
+44 (0)20 7493 6767
asprey.com

Founded in 1781, Asprey does and always did trade in the finer things in life. The current flagship store on New Bond Street, which boasts delicate 19th-century arched shop windows, has been Asprey's home since 1847. It's from here that Asprey have sold luxury dressing cases, accessories, watches and silk scarves to royalty and those with a bit of money to spend.

216 WALDEN CHYMIST

65 Elizabeth St
SW1W 9PJ
Belgravia ⑤
+44 (0)20 7730 0080

Purveyors of toiletries, medicines and everything else you'd expect from a modern pharmacy, Waldon Chymist has been serving the community since 1846. What makes this chemist stand out from the rest of London's is its heritage shopfront. The window, stuffed full of stock, is bookended by lovely signs that advertise its long history.

Well-worn
BOOKSHOPS

217 HATCHARDS

187 Piccadilly
W1J 9LE
Piccadilly ⑤
+44 (0)20 7439 9921
hatchards.co.uk

There are four ever-so-creaky floors filled with hand-picked books to explore in Hatchards. The intimate bookshop, which is the oldest in London (maybe even the United Kingdom), has called the same shop on Piccadilly home for more than two centuries and currently holds three Royal Warrants. And if it's good enough for the Queen, it's more than good enough for us.

218 DAUNT BOOKS MARYLEBONE

83 Marylebone
High St
W1U 4QW
Marylebone ⑥
+44 (0)20 7224 2295
dauntbooks.co.uk/
marylebone

Potentially the prettiest bookshop on the planet, Daunt Books Marylebone resides in a building that dates back to 1910. It was originally built for antiquarian bookseller Francis Edwards. Daunt didn't move in until 1990 but thankfully its elegant Edwardian heritage is still entirely evident in the building's long, oak galleries and glorious stained-glass windows. Visit to stock up on brilliant and beautiful books that you can take away in a trademark Daunt Books tote bag.

219 HEYWOOD HILL

10 Curzon St
W1J 5HH
Mayfair ⑥
+44 (0)20 7629 0647
heywoodhill.com

Writer Nancy Mitford, who penned *The Pursuit of Love* and *Love in a Cold Climate,* worked at Heywood Hill during WWII, and if you're after a delightfully designed set of her lighthearted novels, this is the place to buy it. Opened by George Heywood Hill in 1936, the bookshop, which is set over two floors of a Georgian townhouse, sells a mix of new, old and rare books and remains an entirely charming place to shop.

Stores for
VINTAGE FASHION

---

220 ROKIT

225 Camden High St
NW1 7BU
North ⑭
+44 (0)20 8801 8600
rokit.co.uk

Rokit began as a stall on Camden Market in 1986 selling vintage American denim. Thanks to London's insatiable demand for pre-loved threads, just a few weeks later it became a shop on Camden High Street – and it's been there ever since. There are now Rokit stores in Brick Lane and Covent Garden too, where you can stock up on original and customised vintage clothes from the 1950s right up to the 1990s.

221 RETROMANIA

6 Upper Tachbrook St
SW1V 1SH
Westminster ⑤
+44 (0)20 7630 7406
faracharityshops.org

Dress yourself from a medley of eras gone-by at Retromania, an outpost of charity shop chain Fara that is solely dedicated to vintage. You'll find a well-curated, colourful array of covetable styles, from silk designer scarves to psychedelic mini dresses and beaded ballgowns. It's also a great place to stock up on retro accessories: shoes, bags, even old records.

222 HOUSE OF VINTAGE

4 Cheshire St
E2 6EH
Shoreditch ⑨
+44 (0)20 7739 8142
houseofvintageuk.com

Swing by one of House of Vintage's two East London stores (there's one right by Hackney Central Overground station, too) to stock up on old-timey garms. The store sells high-quality clothes from the 1900s to the 1970s, but the majority of the rails are taken up with items from the 1940s, 1950s and 1960s. Think 1970s dresses, slogan tees, soft sweatshirts and racks of denim. It's a stylish way to improve your sustainability credentials.

223 PAPER DRESS VINTAGE

352a Mare St
E8 1HR
Hackney ⑩
+44 (0)20 8510 0520
paperdress
vintage.co.uk

You'll find hangers full of wearable vintage styles and shapes in a rainbow of shades at Paper Dress Vintage, which has been dressing East Londoners since 2007. Hunt through hand-sourced clothes, shoes and accessories from 1900 to the 1980s. The shop's tailor will help turn your pre-loved find into the perfect fit. There's a coffee shop too if you need a break after all that rummaging, while, at night, the vintage store turns into a buzzy bar and live music venue.

Places to find
ANTIQUES

224 BRICK LANE MARKET

Brick Lane
E1 6QL
Shoreditch ⑨

Head to Brick Lane on a Sunday and the street will be lined with stalls selling secondhand treasures. In true flea market style, you can pick up anything from genuine antique furniture to vintage signs, old china tea sets and well-thumbed books. Take your time wandering through the market to hunt around for gems.

225 THE OLD CINEMA

160 Chiswick High
Road
W4 1PR
West ⑬
+44 (0)20 8995 4166
theoldcinema.co.uk

From a distance, this old movie theatre could still be screening the latest blockbusters, but take a closer look and its current purpose becomes clear. What was once an early-20th-century picturehouse is now a thriving antiques and vintage store, with striking delights spilling out on to Chiswick High Road. Peruse the smaller cabinets for trinkets, Victorian letter racks and unique glassware, before checking out larger items, which on any given day could range from a Georgian writing desk to a mid-century armchair, an art deco ice bucket or an industrial storage cabinet.

226 ALFIES ANTIQUE MARKET

13-25 Church St
NW8 8DT
Marylebone ⑥
+44 (0)20 7723 6066
alfiesantiques.com

Inside a four-floor art deco-style building, you'll find Alfies, London's biggest indoor antiques and vintage market. The arcade, which features around 100 dealers selling retro furniture, clothing, homeware and assorted bric-a-brac, has been buzzing with antique hunters since it opened in 1976. If you're keen to keep spending, Alfies is also surrounded by a number of antiques stores, which are in some cases run by dealers who started out under the market's roof.

227 PORTOBELLO ROAD MARKET

Portobello Road
W11 3DB
West ⑬
+44 (0)20 7361 3001
portobelloroad.co.uk

From secondhand books to bananas, and Caribbean street food to bargain nightdresses, you can buy basically anything from Portobello Road Market, which is open every day except Sunday. If it's antiques you're after though you're going to want to visit on a Friday or, even better, a Saturday, which is when the market is at its biggest and best. The south end of Portobello Road is where you'll find the antiques traders as well as the arcades, which sell a diverse array of antique silver, glass, jewellery and small items of furniture. Arrive before 11.30 am if you're not into crowds.

228 GRAYS

58 Davies St
W1K 5LP
Mayfair ⑥
+44 (0)20 7629 7034
graysantiques.com

A 19th-century former lavatory showroom is where you'll find Grays, an art and antiques centre that was set up in the 1970s. Across two floors, dealers sell fine jewellery, watches, collectables and ornamental antiques. It's a great place to go if you're after advice or are looking to source something specific.

229 WOOD STREET INDOOR MARKET

98-100 Wood St
E17 3HX
Walthamstow ⑪
woodstreetindoor
market.co.uk

Pass under the circus-esque sign and there are 30 traders in snug units to explore at Wood Street Indoor Market. The covered arcade, which sweeps around in a horseshoe-shape, was formerly The Crown Cinema before it closed in 1955. Pop by on the first Sunday of every month to buy retro sweets, antique toys and annuals, vinyl and pre-loved ceramics.

Age-old
ARCADES

---

230 THE ROYAL ARCADE

28 Old Bond St
W1S 4DR
Mayfair ⑥
royalarcade.london

There are a number of elegant and incredibly well-preserved arcades to be found around Mayfair and Piccadilly. Though walking along the refined, covered streets feels like the antithesis of a trip to a huge modern mall, these 19th-century relics were basically London's first shopping centres. Home to watch and jewellery shops as well as Charbonnel et Walker's 145-year-old store, The Royal Arcade is a fine example of the way Victorians liked to splash their cash. Look up to see the glass roof, and colourfully decorated pillars and arches, high above the shop fronts.

230 THE ROYAL ARCADE

231 BURLINGTON ARCADE

51 Piccadilly
W1J 0QJ
Mayfair ⑥
burlingtonarcade.com

If you don't spot the Beadles – the arcade's private police force – in top hats and tails on your way in, it'll soon become apparent how fancy the shops on gated Burlington Arcade are. Floral perfumes and the scent of soft leather shoes waft down its gleaming length, while designer brands line the arcade's interior. Burlington has been welcoming shoppers since 1819 and you can still get your shoes polished in true Victorian style while you're there.

232 PICCADILLY ARCADE

Piccadilly
SW1Y 6NH
Piccadilly ⑤
piccadilly-arcade.com

Don't miss the pretty curved shopfronts or the intricate circular light wells in Piccadilly Arcade, which runs between Piccadilly and Jermyn Street. The handsome Edwardian arcade, which opened in 1909, is home to heritage shoemakers, jewellers, tailors and haberdashers.

233 BRIXTON VILLAGE, RELIANCE ARCADE AND MARKET ROW

Coldharbour Lane
SW9 8PS
South ⑬
wearebrixton
village.co.uk

Brixton's covered markets are a far cry from the hushed shopping arcades in Central London. Constructed between 1925 and 1938, the streets are buzzing and full of life, with bold signage and interiors – notice the Egyptian-influenced east entrance to Reliance Arcade and the arcades' colourful paintwork. The markets became the heart of the Windrush community that settled in Brixton after WWII, bringing with them Caribbean food, music and fashion, culture that ended up shaping the area as well as London as a whole. These days you can buy anything: from metres of West African fabric to fresh fish, a flat white and seasonal small plates at Salon.

Intriguing
SHOPPING STREETS

234 CECIL COURT

WC2N 4EZ
Covent Garden ①
cecilcourt.co.uk

This antiquated passageway just off Charing Cross Road has long been suspected to be one of the places that inspired Diagon Alley in the Harry Potter books — and you don't need magical powers to see why. Laid out in the 17th century, Cecil Court is a retail timewarp, lined with independent stores specialising in coins, silver, stamps, rare maps, art and books. One, Watkins Books, is an esoteric bookshop where you can buy spirituality guides, crystals, talismans and even have a tarot reading.

235 CAMDEN PASSAGE

N1 8EA
Islington ⑧
*camdenpassage
islington.co.uk*

A narrow, car-free lane in Angel, picturesque Camden Passage is known for its dense collection of antiques, vintage and indie shops, pavement cafes and small, open-air markets. It's hidden away from busy Upper Street and stumbling upon it feels like a secret you should keep to yourself. Visit Annie's for lust-worthy vintage dresses, frothy petticoats and silk slips or, to dig around for well-thumbed novels and pre-loved jewels, turn just off the Passage onto Pierrepont Arcade.

236 LEADENHALL MARKET

Gracechurch St
EC3V 1LT
City of London ②
leadenhallmarket.co.uk

Standing on the site of a Roman basilica, the Leadenhall Market of today dates from 1881, though even before the Great Fire of London it was a popular spot to buy meat, fish and cheese. The period roof, cobbles and architecture have all been preserved and it's an attractive spot, especially during the winter when the interconnecting covered market streets are decked out with tiny fir trees and strings of fairy lights. The Victorian shops now house high-street shops and restaurants.

E PEN SHOP

8 & 9

LAMB TAVERN

237 CARNABY STREET

W1F 9PS
Soho ①
carnaby.co.uk

These days it's a hub for independent brands, creative chains and trendy eateries, but Carnaby Street was once the absolute hottest shopping street in the city. Just a short walk away from the chaos of Oxford Street, colourful Carnaby was the birthplace of the Swinging Sixties, a favourite of Jimi Hendrix, The Beatles and The Rolling Stones, and a meeting place for rockers, mods, punks and skinheads alike.

238 KING'S ROAD

SW3 5ES
Chelsea ④
kingsroadlondon.com

Stretching through the heart of Chelsea, this road got its name because it used to be a private route for King Charles II to take to Kew. Fast-forward a few centuries and the King's Road became a hub of creativity and culture. Mary Quant, the fashion designer famous for her miniskirts, opened a store on the King's Road in 1955 while Vivienne Westwood ran a store called SEX during the 1970s that basically helped spawn punk. It's lost its edge over recent years, but there was a time when strutting these pavements would have been the pinnacle of cool.

239 SAVILE ROW

W1S 2ER
Mayfair ⑥
savilerowbespoke.com

Since the early 19th century, Savile Row has been the home of bespoke British tailoring and the street continues to kit well-heeled customers out in the finest suits. Prince Charles buys his from Anderson & Sheppard, who have been on Savile Row since 1906. Along the road, you'll find more historic businesses, like Norton & Sons, who have made suits for royalty and three US presidents. There's also Davies & Son, which was established in 1803, and Dege & Skinner, a family-run tailoring house which first opened on the Row in 1865.

Iconic
DEPARTMENT STORES

240 FORTNUM & MASON

181 Piccadilly
W1A 1ER
Piccadilly ⑤
+44 (0)20 7734 8040
fortnumandmason.com

A resplendent food and homewares department store, Fortnum & Mason has been drawing crowds to 181 Piccadilly since 1707. As soon as you step inside the historic shop it's clear you're somewhere rather special – there's something about the plush red carpets, creaking grand staircase, elegant circular atrium and the sea of the store's trademark shade (eau de nil) stretching out in front of you. First and foremost, Fortnum's is famed for its luxe or exotic foodstuffs – it invented the Scotch egg, introduced Heinz baked beans to Britain and won first prize as importers of dried fruits and dessert goods at 1851's Great Exhibition, so it's no surprise that it remains an ace place to stock up on ready-to-eat treats. Follow in the footsteps of 18th-century travellers, explorers and picnickers and fill an iconic F&M wicker hamper up to the brim with tea, biscuits, preserves and other edible delights.

241 HARRODS

87-135 Brompton
Road
SW1X 7XL
Kensington ④
+44 (0)20 7730 1234
harrods.com

What is now one of London's most prestigious department stores, filled with high-end and designer products, started life as a tiny grocery shop in 1835. The grand façade that exists today was constructed around the turn of the century, at about the same time that Harrods installed Britain's very first escalator. It's hard to imagine now, but when it was first introduced there was an attendant waiting at the top ready to offer brandy to anyone feeling a little shaken by the newfangled experience.

242 SELFRIDGES

400 Oxford St
W1A 1AB
Marylebone ⑥
+44 (0)20 7160 6222
selfridges.com

The doors to Selfridges were first flung open by American millionaire Harry Selfridge in 1909. His huge store, modelled on American superstores, was designed to be the first of its kind in England, complete with 130 departments, creative window displays and a thrilling, theatrical atmosphere. Much of his vision endures and shopping in Selfridges remains a unique experience. Inside its 100-year-old shell, the bustling store continues to be innovative, working with artists and hosting pop-ups. These days there is a cinema, piercing studio and even in-store psychics for shoppers in need of some spiritual healing.

243 LIBERTY LONDON

243 LIBERTY LONDON

Regent St
W1B 5AH
Soho ①
+44 (0)20 7734 1234
libertylondon.com

Gorgeous Liberty London was built in Tudor revival style in the 1920s, using the timbers from two ancient battleships, *HMS Impregnable* and *HMS Hindustan* – though the shop had been selling exotic and unusual fabrics, ornaments and objects for almost 50 years already when it moved into its stunning new home. Creative and artistic, Liberty continues to thrill shoppers with its clever curation of homewares, beauty and fashion. Don't leave without walking around the enormous, beamed atrium at the heart of the store.

244 HARVEY NICHOLS

109-125
Knightsbridge
SW1X 7RJ
Belgravia ⑤
+44 (0)20 7235 5000
harveynichols.com

This glamourous store opened in 1831 as a linen shop in a terraced house on the corner of Knightsbridge and Sloane Street. It expanded and expanded until Harvey Nichols took up the entire block between Seville Street and Sloane Street. Soon the buildings were demolished and by 1894 the grand purpose-built store you can visit today, for cutting-edge fashion and luxury brands, stood in their place.

245 HAMLEYS

188-196 Regent St
W1B 5BT
Soho ①
+44 (0)37 1704 1977
hamleys.com

The toys have definitely changed over the years, but in essence Hamleys is the same as it was when it first opened, as Noah's Ark, in 1760. The store, selling wooden toys and rag dolls, was such a success that it expanded, opening the seven-floor Regent Street store it resides in today in 1881. One of the oldest and largest toy shops in the world, Hamleys continues to welcome wide-eyed children through its historic doors every day of the week.

ROWLEY'S

FOOD

Established
BAKERIES

---

246 PAUL ROTHE & SON

35 Marylebone Lane
W1U 2NN
Marylebone ⑥
+44 (0)20 7935 6783

Check out the shelves piled high with traditional jams, marmalades and chutney in this vintage spot – it's like an enormous, delicious pantry. Run by the generations of the Rothe family since 1900, this sandwich shop is pretty to look at, but it's not all style over substance. Order a sandwich (any filling goes), watch as it's whipped up in front of you, and then devour it while sat at one of the mid-century Formica tables.

247 MAISON BERTAUX

28 Greek St
W1D 5DQ
Soho ①
+44 (0)20 7437 6007
maisonbertaux.com

A higgledy-piggledy patisserie and tearoom, Maison Bertaux is set over two floors of a Soho townhouse, with more tables spilling out onto the pavement and into the ground floor of the building next door. Service is a little chaotic, but it's part of the cafe's charm. The spot has been serving up generous slices of tart, lavish cream cakes and elegant pastries since 1871, when Monsieur Bertaux arrived in London to share his French recipes.

248 RINKOFF BAKERY

224 Jubilee St
E1 3BS
East ⑪
+44 (0)20 7790 1050
rinkoffbakery.co.uk

This old-school East End bakery has been in the same family for over a century. It was established by Jewish baker Hyman Rinkoff, who travelled from Kiev to London to set up his baking business in 1911. These days Rinkoffs still trades in traditional bakes like *challah* breads, *babka* and buns, as well as more modern creations like rainbow bagels and crodoughs (that's halfway between a croissant and a doughnut fyi.) They run a deli on nearby 79 Vallance Road, too.

249 DUNNS BAKERY

6 The Broadway
N8 9SN
North ⑭
+44 (0)20 8340 1614
dunns-bakery.co.uk

Much-loved Crouch End bakery Dunns has been in the Freeman family since the 1820s, when Robert Freeman set up shop in Highgate. They've been baking bread, cakes and piles of sweet treats in their current premises since 1850, and the place is currently run by Lewis, the sixth generation of bakers. Spot the blue wooden doors to the right of the shop windows – they would have once been used by a horse and delivery cart.

250 BRICK LANE'S BAGEL SHOPS

E1 6SB
Shoreditch ⑨

If you're after a bagel in London, there's no question you want to head to Brick Lane. Whether you visit the yellow shop or the white shop? Well, that's a trickier decision. Practically neighbours, these two bagel shops both serve up brilliant boiled and baked bagels, stuffed full of cream cheese or thick slices of salt beef and mustard, for bargain prices. Both are open 24 hours a day – Beigel Bake hasn't changed its recipe since 1974, while Beigel Shop has been serving customers since 1855.

Classic
FISH AND CHIP *shops*

---

251 ROCK & SOLE PLAICE

47 Endell St
WC2H 9AJ
Covent Garden ①
+44 (0)20 7836 3785
rockandsoleplaice.com

It got its clever name in the 1970s, but Rock & Sole Plaice originates from 1871 when a restaurant opened at 47 Endell Street to serve fish and chips to local market workers. At the time, it was only the third fish and chip shop to open in London, though the fried pairing is now considered a classic English dish. Swing by to sample the traditional meal or mix things up with some of the more recent additions to the menu, like veggie-friendly crispy coated camembert with chips.

252 THE GOLDEN HIND

71A-73 Marylebone
Lane
W1U 2PN
Marylebone ⑥
+44 (0)20 7486 3644
goldenhind
restaurant.com

Open since 1914, this traditional fish and chip joint is one of London's best. Stick with the classics served in pleasingly generous portions, or opt for something a little lighter – you can have your fish steamed rather than encased in crispy batter if you prefer. The classic British desserts – think rhubarb crumble, spotted dick and syrup sponge with custard – are well worth ordering, too.

253 THE FRYER'S DELIGHT

19 Theobalds Road
WC1X 8SL
Bloomsbury ⑦
+44 (0)20 7405 4114

This spot first opened in 1958 and after a quick look at its retro interiors and vintage sign you won't doubt it. It's barely changed since then, still serving up simple grub – pies, battered cod, mushy peas and pickled cucumbers – in simple surroundings.

Traditional
TEAROOMS

---

254 PALM COURT
AT: THE RITZ
150 Piccadilly
W1J 9BR
St James's ⑤
+44 (0)20 7300 2345
theritzlondon.com

There aren't many things more traditionally English than afternoon tea – the meal, typically served on tiered plates, is said to have been dreamt up in the mid 19th century by a duchess, who was fed up of the long wait between lunch and dinner – and there aren't many places more spectacular to 'take tea' than at The Ritz. There's a smart dress code and a live pianist to accompany your visit. Feasting on delicious delicacies surrounded by mirrored walls and elaborate floral displays is old-school glamour at its best.

255 THE GARDEN CAFÉ
AT: THE V&A
Cromwell Road
SW7 2RL
Kensington ④
+44 (0)20 7942 2000
vam.ac.uk

If you need a pick-me-up after exploring the V&A's many exhibitions and gallery spaces, there's nowhere better than the Garden Café. When it opened in 1856, it was the world's first museum restaurant, serving tea, buns and hot meals to weary visitors. It's still a great place to refuel today. Pick up a generous wedge of sponge and a pot of Earl Grey to enjoy in the bright and highly decorated Gamble Room, whose dazzling tiles, bold arches and ceramic ceiling were unveiled in 1868. Another of the original refreshment rooms was designed by a young William Morris. To sit surrounded by one of his earliest patterns, pre-book a historically accurate Victorian-style afternoon tea, currently served every Friday.

256 PALM COURT

AT: THE LANGHAM
1-C Portland Place
W1B 1JA
Marylebone ⑥
+44 (0)20 7636 1000
langhamhotels.com

Charles Dickens and Sir Arthur Conan Doyle are known to have been fans of this hotel, which claims to be the first hotel ever to serve afternoon tea. Whether or not that's true, it can't be denied that The Langham knows what it's doing. It's been serving tea, dainty sandwiches and pretty pastries in the elegant Palm Court since 1865.

257 THE FOYER AND READING ROOM

AT: CLARIDGE'S
Brook St
W1K 4HR
Mayfair ⑥
+44 (0)20 7107 8886
claridges.co.uk

With its gilded columns, grand proportions and original art deco mirrors, the 1930s Foyer and Reading Room in Claridge's has been charming visitors for more than 150 years. After you've devoured a pile of tiny sandwiches, warm fruit scones with Cornish clotted cream and handmade sweets, and sipped a cup of the hotel's bespoke tea blend in elegant striped china, you'll be surprised to step onto a 21st-century street when you leave.

258 DIAMOND JUBILEE SALON

AT: FORTNUM & MASON
181 Piccadilly
W1A 1ER
Piccadilly ⑤
+44 (0)20 7734 8040
fortnumandmason.com

Climb to the top floor of Fortnum & Mason's delightful Piccadilly store and you're in for a treat. The Tea Salon has been making a good brew since the 1920s, but was done up in elegant, vintage style to mark the Queen's – you guessed it – diamond jubilee. Visit to sample Fortnum's famous teas (there are more than 50 blends on the menu) on their historic premises. You can order your afternoon tea sweet or savoury – or pimped with one of F&M's classic Scotch eggs.

259 OSCAR WILDE LOUNGE

AT: HOTEL CAFÉ ROYAL
68 Regent St
W1B 4DY
Soho ①
+44 (0)20 7406 3310
hotelcaferoyal.com

If you take afternoon tea at the Hotel Café Royal, you'll be served in an ornate mirrored room, which dates back to 1865. Named after one famous former patron, the room is said to have been visited by David Bowie, Mick Jagger, The Beatles and Elizabeth Taylor, as well as Wilde himself. While the practice of afternoon tea is traditional, here you can expect clever twists on old classics.

Vintage CAFES and COFFEE SHOPS

---

260 E. PELLICCI

332 Bethnal Green Rd
E2 0AG
East ⑪
+44 (0)20 7739 4873
epellicci.co.uk

A classic East End caff, E. Pellicci has been brewing tea and frying eggs since 1900. You can also get grilled sandwiches, pasta dishes and hearty lunches here, but its Full English, served all day, is what the Italian cafe is famous for. Spot the stunning shop front and ornate, art deco wood panelled interior, which was added after WWII and is now Grade II-listed.

261 BAR ITALIA

22 Frith St
W1D 4RF
Soho ①
+44 (0)20 7437 4520
baritaliasoho.co.uk

Serving strong coffees, pastries, snacks and Aperols from 7 am until 5 am, this small, Italian cafe first opened in 1949 and has gone on to become a Soho institution. Many of Bar Italia's original features remain intact, like the red and white Formica bar. It quickly became a social spot for London's Italian community after opening, and continues to welcome loved regulars and Soho personalities today.

262 REGENCY CAFE

17-19 Regency St
SW1P 4BY
Westminster ⑤
+44 (0)20 7821 6596

You can't help but feel transported back to the 1940s in Regency Cafe, a quietly popular greasy spoon that's been serving up bargain breakfasts and proper old-fashioned English food since 1946. The retro spot has a striking black exterior and windows edged with frilly gingham curtains, while its tiled interiors have hardly changed over the decades, making it a magnet for filmmakers.

263 **THE ORIGINAL MAIDS OF HONOUR**

288 Kew Road
TW9 3DU
West ⑬
+44 (0)20 8940 2752
theoriginalmaidsof honour.co.uk

Named after Maids of Honour tarts, which were said to be King Henry VIII's favourites, this traditional cafe, just outside Kew Gardens, can trace its roots back to the early 18th century. The cafe moved to its current spot in 1860, though the little mock-Tudor building dates from the 1940s after the original was badly bombed during WWII. That wholesome, post-war atmosphere can still be felt when sitting in the dining room today, eating a traditional pie for 'luncheon' or snacking on their special set tea – like afternoon tea, but with pies, quiches and sausage rolls, too.

264 **ALPINO**

97 Chapel Market
N1 9EY
Islington ⑧
+44 (0)20 7837 8330

This simple cafe first opened its doors in the late 1950s and it's much the same today. Lively and always busy with speedy service, Alpino serves up generous portions of classic Italian-English food for good-value prices. Stop by for a filling, traditional fry-up or an Alpino club sandwich: ciabatta stuffed with chicken escalope, mozzarella and Napoli sauce.

RETRO
eateries

---

265 OSLO COURT
Charlbert St
NW8 7EN
North ⑭
+44 (0)20 7722 8795
oslocourt
restaurant.co.uk

Run by Tony Sanchez and his family, this total time warp, set in the ground floor of a 1930s block of flats, has changed very little since it opened. That was in 1982, but the place is pure 1970s. The restaurant is all draped curtains, salmon pink tablecloths and old-school vibes. Order rich, retro delights like melon with Parma ham or deep-fried mushrooms drowning in garlic butter to start, followed by a meaty main swimming in sauces spiked with wine and cream. Portions here are generous – the vegetable and potato sides just keep coming – but make sure you leave room for dessert, served from a trolley stacked high with tarts, mousses and meringues in the corner of the room. Show any indecision and staff will choose for you, which is no bad thing.

266 INDIA CLUB
143-145 Strand
WC2R 1JA
Covent Garden ①
+44 (0)20 7836 4880
theindiaclub.co.uk

You could easily walk right by this curry house, hidden up a flight of stairs off a small doorway on the Strand. The bar, lounge and Indian restaurant (one of the UK's oldest), where you can order delicious South Indian dishes, feels frozen in time. You'll find the same simple furniture and artwork that was installed when India Club was set up almost 60 years ago by the India League as 'a symbol of post-independence friendship'. A social meeting place as well as a restaurant, this place became an important hub for London's burgeoning Asian community.

267 CIAO BELLA

**86-90 Lamb's
Conduit St
WC1N 3LZ
Bloomsbury ⑦
+44 (0)20 7242 4119**
*ciaobella
restaurant.co.uk*

Packed and loud, with live music and raised voices, Ciao Bella is a perfect example of what London's dining scene was like in the 1980s. This old-fashioned, lively Italian restaurant hasn't budged since it first opened, and judging by the crowds that arrive every evening, it's working for them. Service is quick, staff no-nonsense and portions (order pasta, always pasta) are enormous. An evening here might verge on the chaotic but it's part of this retro spot's appeal.

267 **CIAO BELLA**

268 LANGAN'S BRASSERIE

Stratton St
W1J 8LB
Mayfair ⑥
+44 (0)20 7491 8822
langansbrasserie.com

Established in 1976 by flamboyant restaurateur Peter Langan and acting icon Michael Caine, Langan's was a celebrity favourite during the 1980s. The French-English cuisine and rowdy atmosphere attracted stars like Marlon Brando, Jack Nicholson and David Hockney. Neither the walls, which are studded with impressive artworks, nor the menu has changed very much over the last few decades. Order retro dishes like liver and bacon or snails in puff pastry to really embrace the atmosphere.

269 JOE ALLEN RESTAURANT

2 Burleigh St
WC2E 7PX
Covent Garden ①
+44 (0)20 7836 0651
joeallen.co.uk

1970s vibes abound at this West End joint, which has been dishing out New York-style food since it opened in 1977. The exposed-brick walls are covered in photographs of famous faces and plastered with posters for productions gone by, while neat white and red checked tablecloths adorn the tables. Eat the pre-theatre set menu, while a pianist tinkles away in the background – or order Joe Allen's not-so-secret off-menu burger.

270 ROWLEY'S

113 Jermyn St
SW1Y 6HJ
St James's ⑤
+44 (0)20 7930 2707
rowleys.co.uk

Serving since 1976, this old-school spot, in the building where Wall's butchers (the company famous for its sausages) was established, is rather special. Rowley's gleams thanks to perfectly preserved vintage tiles, polished mirrors and the curvy gold lettering in its enormous windows. The atmosphere is a little formal and fancy, while the menu is reminiscent of the restaurant's 1970s inception. You'll find the likes of prawn cocktail, smoked salmon on buttered brown bread and chicken supreme. Order the house entrecôte steak, which comes topped with butter sauce on a table burner with unlimited fries – you won't regret it.

Well-preserved
PIE AND MASH SHOPS

_____

271 F. COOKE

150 Hoxton St
N1 6SH
Hackney ⑩
+44 (0)20 7729 7718

London's original fast-food joints, pie and mash shops are as much a part of London history as red phone boxes and the royal family. But the restaurants, which have been around since the mid 19th century, are in decline. Only a handful of traditional spots remain, still serving cheap, cockney-style pastry pies with mashed potatoes and a green, parsley liquor. One of them is F. Cooke, run by a family who opened their first pie shop in the 1860s. Despite the recent closure of their 120-year-old Broadway Market branch, F. Cooke in Hoxton is still going strong, serving up meat pies (you can get vegan ones, too, these days) and hearty cups of rosy lee to tourists and loyal regulars.

272 ARMENTS
PIE AND MASH

7-9 Westmoreland Rd
SE17 2AX
South ⑫
+44 (0)20 7703 4974
armentspie
andmash.com

Arments have been in this spot on Westmoreland Road since 1979, but their history goes back as far as 1914. Still family-run and serving up old-school pies using the original recipe, the South London institution is the place to go for flaky pastry and creamy mash. Spot the blue plaque on the side of the building, which was installed to mark the much-loved shop's 100th anniversary.

273 M. MANZE

87 Tower Bridge
Road
SE1 4TW
South ⑫
+44 (0)20 7407 2985
manze.co.uk

The first of a small chain of pie and mash shops set up by
Italian Michael Manze, M. Manze on Tower Bridge Road
opened in 1902. The interior of the Grade II-listed shop is
almost exactly as it would have been back then – check out
the green, cream and pink floral tiling, marble-topped tables
and terrazzo floor. At one point there were 14 M. Manze pie
and mash shops in London, but times have changed. Now just
three shops remain – but you can order Manze's pie, mash and
eels on Deliveroo, too.

274 THE JELLIED EEL

AT: MANZE'S PIE & MASH
76 High St
E17 7LD
Walthamstow ⑪
+44 (0)20 8520 2855
thejelliedeel.com

London's appetite for pies and eel might be waning, but
Manze's has a plan. By day, this shop serves up traditional pie,
mash and eel in an untouched 1929 setting (just look at the
tiled walls, dark wooden booths and decorative tin-panelled
ceiling). By night it's a bar, where cocktails, croquetas and
small plates are on the menu. The Jellied Eel, which is open
after-hours on Fridays and Saturdays, makes use of the shop's
stunning Grade II-listed decor as well as a courtyard garden
out the back.

271 F. COOKE

...es light upon all hands playing in linen fields

The OLDEST RESTAURANTS
in London

—————

275 RULES

35 Maiden Lane
WC2E 7LB
Covent Garden ①
+44 (0)20 7836 5314
rules.co.uk

Established in 1798, Rules calls itself the oldest restaurant in the city – and it certainly trades on that impressive heritage. Charles Dickens and H.G. Wells are known to have eaten here, and inside, with its red velvet booths, plush patterned carpets and richly decorated walls, it feels like a time capsule. The truth is the restaurant has evolved with the times – you can order a Duchess of Cambridge cocktail, for example – but when it comes to the food tradition prevails. Expect steamed pies, game and oysters finished off with Rules' golden syrup sponge.

276 SIMPSON'S TAVERN

Ball Court
at 38½ Cornhill
EC3V 9DR
City of London ②
+44 (0)20 7626 9985
simpsonstavern.co.uk

Need somewhere to rest your top hat? That won't be a problem at Simpson's Tavern, where each intimate wooden booth is topped with a hat rack. The layout of this charming Grade II-listed spot, found down an olde-worlde alleyway in the City, hasn't changed since it opened in 1757. Only open midweek for lunch and breakfast (Tuesday–Friday), it's popular with local city workers enjoying long boozy breaks – and anyone with a taste for filling English fare. Order Edwardian pork chops or poached salmon with hefty sides of mash and creamy spinach. Just leave room for the sizable sausage that is offered as a traditional side with everything on the menu.

277 SIMPSON'S IN THE STRAND

100 Strand
WC2R 0EW
Covent Garden ①
+44 (0)20 7420 2111
simpsonsin thestrand.co.uk

Traditional Simpson's in the Strand is one of the oldest spots in London, having opened in 1828. Once you've stepped across the pretty threshold (look up at the tiling and gilded sign on your way in) you're greeted with wood panelled walls, leather chairs and pristine tablecloths. Want the full, theatrical Simpson's experience? Order rib of beef or saddle of lamb and it'll be served at your table from the carving trolley.

278 SWEETINGS

39 Queen Victoria St
EC4N 4SA
City of London ②
+44 (0)20 7248 3062
sweetings restaurant.co.uk

Sweetings is a seafood, lunch-only restaurant – and has been around since 1830. That's when the original spot opened, though it's been in its current premises for a little over a century. Inside you'll find mosaiced flooring, wood panels and touches of blue that match the vintage exterior, as well as waistcoat-wearing waiters and a side order of serious nostalgia. Drinks are served in silver tankards, everything seems to come with buttered bread and the menu is peppered with soothing old-fashioned dishes like fish pie and jam roll.

279 SCOTT'S

20 Mount St
W1K 2HE
Mayfair ⑥
+44 (0)20 7495 7309
scotts-restaurant.com

With roots that go back as far as 1851, Scott's is a historic, fine dining destination decked out with elegant, art deco-inspired interiors. It's been an expert in seafood since it started life as an oyster warehouse. To do Scott's properly (and if you're up for a blowout), order Jersey Pearl English oysters followed by grilled lobster with garlic butter and wash it all down with a glass or two of champagne.

280 WILTONS

55 Jermyn St
SW1Y 6LX
St James's ⑤
+44 (0)20 7629 9955
wiltons.co.uk

With beginnings as a shellfish-mongers in 1742, Wiltons has been serving traditional English fare as a restaurant since the early 19th century. It moved to its current spot on Jermyn Street in the 1980s, but retained its old-school charm. Popular with those who enjoy the finer things in life, it feels a little like a private members' club but, don't worry, as long as they can pay their bill at the end, anyone is welcome to eat Stilton souffles and smoked eel in their plush dining room.

281 J. SHEEKEY

28-32 St Martin's
Court
WC2N 4AL
Covent Garden ①
+44 (0)20 7240 2565
j-sheekey.co.uk

More than 100 years old, J. Sheekey serves up classic fish dishes in late-Victorian surroundings. The place oozes old-fashioned glamour, its bold red façade pressed up against Wyndham's Theatre in the West End. Seeing a play nearby? Drop in afterwards to take advantage of the fish pie and other delights on the late-night, post-theatre set menu.

FINE DINING

in fine surroundings

---

282 THE WOLSELEY

160 Piccadilly
W1J 9EB
Piccadilly ⑤
+44 (0)20 7499 6996
thewolseley.com

Restaurants don't get much more impressive than
The Wolseley, a European-style grand cafe which resides
in a former 1920s car showroom. The eatery serves elegant
food all day long, from Scottish steaks to French stews
and German desserts. But it's the building – marble pillars,
sweeping archways and the geometric floor preserved
from the space's 1920s heydey – that makes a meal here
truly special.

283 BIBENDUM

AT: MICHELIN HOUSE
81 Fulham Road
SW3 6RD
Chelsea ④
+44 (0)20 7581 5817
bibendum.co.uk

With colourful glazed tiles, ornamental ironwork, stained-
glass windows and decorative turrets that look like little
stacks of tires, Michelin House has to be one of the most
interesting buildings in London. Grade II-listed, it originally
opened in 1911 as the Michelin Tyre Company's UK
headquarters and tyre depot. These days it's where you
can find Bibendum, a fancy French restaurant named after
the Michelin Man himself.

284 L'ESCARGOT

48 Greek St
W1D 4EF
Soho ①
+44 (0)20 7439 7474
lescargot.co.uk

Established in 1896 by Frenchman Georges Gaudin, L'Escargot moved to its current home – an elegant early-18th-century townhouse decked out in flamboyant style – in 1927, where apparently Gaudin ran a snail farm in the basement. That's no longer the case but the oldest French restaurant in London is still the place to go for retro French cuisine, and really good snails.

285 THE QUALITY CHOP HOUSE

88-94 Farringdon
Road
EC1R 3EA
Clerkenwell ⑧
+44 (0)20 7278 1452
thequality
chophouse.com

Stop by to eat something wonderfully old-fashioned, like beef mince on dripping toast, and admire the checkerboard floor, dark wooden booths, timber wall panels and retro signage – reading 'Progressive Working Class Caterers' and 'London's Noted Cup of Tea' – while you're at it. They are all Grade II-listed original features from The Quality Chop House's Victorian beginnings. The current restaurant opened in 2012, but there's been one here since 1869 when The Quality Chop House opened to serve Farringdon's local working-class residents.

286 BRASSERIE ZÉDEL

20 Sherwood St
W1F 7ED
Soho ①
+44 (0)20 7734 4888
brasseriezedel.com

Brasserie Zédel is deceptive. At first it appears to simply be a charming, petite Parisian-style cafe (and you could leave none the wiser) but venture downstairs and the space opens out into an enormous, authentic art deco dining room. Originally The Grill Room of the Regent Palace Hotel, the basement is all symmetrical marble columns, brass rails, gold cornicing and gleaming mirrors. Pull a chair up to one of those pink tablecloths to order French dishes like boeuf bourguignon and tarte Tatin in an otherwordly, Wes Anderson-esque setting.

THE CHURCHILL ARMS

DRINK

Vintage
WINE BARS

287 GORDON'S WINE BAR

47 Villiers St
WC2N 6NE
Covent Garden ①
+44 (0)20 7930 1408
gordonswinebar.com

London bars don't get more atmospheric than Gordon's. It's set in a vaulted candlelit cellar, thought to date back to the early 17th century, where damp stone walls are covered in faded newspaper clippings and aged memorabilia. Nothing here appears to have changed since the wine bar first opened in 1890, when writer Rudyard Kipling rented a room in the building upstairs – and that's the way the Gordon family (who took over in the 1970s and aren't actually related to founder Angus Gordon) like it. Apparently the late Luis Gordon insisted even cobwebs be preserved during a revamp in the 1990s. These days rustic Gordon's continues to only serve wine, with plates of cheese, bread and salad for the peckish. All the cosy, cobwebby corners taken? The outside terrace is normally buzzing whatever the weather.

288 THE OLDE WINE SHADES

6 Martin Lane
EC4R 0DP
City of London ②
+44 (0)20 7626 6876
elvino.co.uk/bars/the-olde-wine-shades

It's had something of a modern makeover inside, but this historic bar is actually considered to be the oldest in the City. It's one of only a few buildings in this part of town which survived 1666's Great Fire of London. Now run by wine bar chain El Vino – which itself is fairly historic, being founded in 1879 – it's a great spot for sampling Spanish, Portuguese and South American wines with tapas.

289 LE BEAUJOLAIS

25 Litchfield St
WC2H 9NJ
Covent Garden ①
+44 (0)20 7836 2955
lebeaujolais.london

You can sip a chilled glass of French red, with a plate of fromage, pâté and baguette, at this surprising bar, tucked away between Covent Garden, Chinatown and the theatres of Shaftesbury Avenue. The loud and intimate ground-floor space, with rustic tables pushed close together and ties and tankards dangling from the ceiling, is London's oldest French wine bar. There's also a members' club restaurant in the basement that's been serving up French classics by invitation only since the 1970s.

289 LE BEAUJOLAIS

The OLDEST PUBS
in London

---

290 THE MAYFLOWER

117 Rotherhithe St
SE16 4NF
South ⑫
+44 (0)20 7237 4088
mayflowerpub.co.uk

The oldest pub in London? Thanks to fires, bombs, rebuilds, redesigns and a lack of definitive records, there are a handful that can legitimately vie for the title, but no clear way of working out which one is actually the oldest. The Mayflower, a creaky, low-beamed riverside pub with a compellingly nostalgic vibe, is a solid contender. One drink in a candlelit corner and it's easy to fall for the charm of this pub, which claims to have been built in the 16th century. If the weather allows, grab a table on the jetty deck where you can look out on the spot that the *Mayflower* ship supposedly set sail from, laiden with pilgrims headed for the Americas, in 1620.

291 THE PROSPECT OF WHITBY

57 Wapping Wall
E1W 3SH
East ⑪
+44 (0)20 7481 1095
greeneking-pubs.co.uk

This riverside boozer dates from around 1520, though much of the building you can see today is from the early 19th century. Lean on the pewter bar, marvel at the 400-year-old flagstone floor or tuck yourself away in a dark and cosy corner. Out the back the Thames laps at the pub's outdoor terrace. It would be totally idyllic if not for the replica noose flapping in the wind, a nod to riverside executions that used to take place in Wapping.

292 YE OLDE MITRE

1 Ely Court
EC1N 6SJ
Holborn ①
+44 (0)20 7405 4751
*yeoldemitre
holborn.co.uk*

There's something otherworldly about stepping down
an alleyway and stumbling upon Ye Olde Mitre beneath
a canopy of twinkling lights. The tiny pub is thought to
have been founded in 1546, though today's building dates
from the 18th and 20th centuries. Inside, two spaces with
open fireplaces and cosy vibes are snug up against a central
bar. Spot the trunk of what is believed to be a cherry tree
in the corner of the front bar. The tree marked the
boundary between land belonging to the Bishop of Ely
and Sir Christopher Hatton in Elizabethan times.

293 THE GEORGE INN

77 Borough High St
SE1 1NH
South Bank ③
+44 (0)20 7407 2056
*nationaltrust.org.uk/
georgeinn*

This special spot is London's last remaining galleried inn.
Rebuilt in 1677, on the site of an even older 16th-century
inn, the Grade I-listed, National Trust-owned building is
the only pub of this type to survive the Blitz. Settle down for
an evening here in the coaching inn's sunny courtyard or in
one of the higgledy-piggledy building's atmospheric rooms.
You'll feel like you're in Shakespeare's London. And the
Southwark local may actually have drunk in the original inn –
you never know.

294 YE OLDE CHESHIRE CHEESE

145 Fleet St
EC4A 2BU
Holborn ①
+44 (0)20 7353 6170

Rebuilt in 1667, shortly after the Great Fire of London, this
dark, historic drinking den feels like a portal back to another
time. A sign on the way in reads 'you are entering another
century' while reminding punters the pub is a tech-free zone.
Entry is down a narrow, unassuming alleyway. Once inside
you'll find wood panels, open fires, whitewashed stone cellars,
a maze of rooms connected by low-lit (and low-ceilinged)
passageways and plenty of quiet corners. Little imagination
is needed to see why Charles Dickens, Arthur Conan Doyle,
Lord Tennyson and P.G. Wodehouse were drawn to drinking
in this pub.

295 THE SEVEN STARS

53 Carey St
WC2A 2JB
Holborn ①
+44 (0)20 7242 8521
thesevenstars1602.co.uk

Established in 1602, this narrow, charismatic spot is another that can lay claim to being one of London's oldest pubs. Inside, the interiors are Victorian, with rustic, retro flair. Spot hops hanging from the ceiling, checked tablecloths and vintage posters on the walls. Keep your eyes peeled for the pub cat, too.

296 THE GRAPES

76 Narrow St
E14 8BP
East ⑪
+44 (0)20 7987 4396
thegrapes.co.uk

The building is early 18th century, but The Grapes reckons it can trace its history back to 1583. An atmospheric drinking den, right on the water's edge, it's low-lit and narrow inside, opening out onto a little terrace teetering over the Thames. The spot has more than one celebrity connection. It's thought to have charmed Charles Dickens, who references the place in his novel *Our Mutual Friend,* while Sir Ian McKellen is currently one of the pub's leaseholders and has been spotted at the pub quiz on more than one occasion.

Grand
HOTEL BARS

297 AMERICAN BAR

AT: THE SAVOY
Strand
WC2R 0EZ
Covent Garden ①
+44 (0)20 7420 2111
thesavoylondon.com

The oldest surviving cocktail bar in the country, the American Bar has been mixing up alcoholic masterpieces since 1893. This place isn't stuck in the past – it was recently awarded a World's Best Bar accolade – but the sense of history here is palpable. The art deco bar is legendary and is known to have welcomed Fred Astaire, Frank Sinatra, Marilyn Monroe and countless others – check out the framed photographs at the entrance. Expect a regularly changing rosta of innovative cocktails, soundtracked by a live pianist and served in timeless surroundings.

298 DUKES BAR

AT: DUKES LONDON
35 St James's Place
SW1A 1NY
St James's ⑤
+44 (0)20 7491 4840
dukeshotel.com/
dukes-bar

This heritage hotel, near St James's Palace and the old-fashioned shops of Jermyn Street, dates from the early 20th century and trades on its traditional appeal. Dukes Bar is no different – it's like the setting of a black and white movie and things only get more cinematic once you order a martini, served tableside by a mixologist in a sharp white suit. This place, a favourite of author Ian Fleming, is said to have provided the inspiration for James Bond's 'shaken not stirred' tipple of choice.

300 CHAMPAGNE BAR AT KETTNER'S

299 CONNAUGHT BAR

AT: THE CONNAUGHT
Carlos Place
W1K 2AL
Mayfair ⑥
+44 (0)20 7499 7070
the-connaught.co.uk

Timeless glamour is on the menu at the Connaught Bar. It might not be as historic as its hotel setting, but the shimmering space evokes a sense of 1920s style with its cubist and art deco design flourishes. Order twists on classic old-fashioned drinks. You can't go wrong with a personalised Connaught martini, ceremonially served at your table from their famous martini trolley.

300 CHAMPAGNE BAR

AT: KETTNER'S
29 Romilly St
W1D 5HP
Soho ①
+44 (0)20 7734 5650
kettners.com

First opened in 1867 by August Kettner as a French restaurant, lounge and champagne bar, Kettner's became a much-loved Soho institution, visited by the likes of Oscar Wilde, Agatha Christie and Winston Churchill. It's now part of Soho House's empire, its once-famous restaurant a private members' club and its upstairs rooms kitted out in the club's trademark sumptuous style, with 1920s inspired interiors. The champagne bar, though, remains open to the public and has been gloriously restored to its glamourous heyday where you can enjoy champagne martinis and classic serves in a stunning setting. Check out the sweet circular bar and original mosaic floor.

HAUNTED
pubs

---

301 THE TEN BELLS
84 Commercial St
E1 6LY
Spitalfields ⑨
+44 (0)20 7247 7532
tenbells.com

A classic East End boozer in the heart of Spitalfields, The Ten Bells has been a popular place for a post-work pint since 1666, though the present building is around 150 years old. The eye-catching original Victorian tiling is reason enough to pop by, though if you like a ghost story The Ten Bells has another selling point. As well as connections to Jack the Ripper – a number of his victims are said to have visited the pub on the night they died – the pub is supposedly haunted by the spirits of a former murdered landlord and a 19th-century baby.

302 THE SPANIARDS INN
Spaniards Road
NW3 7JJ
North ⑭
+44 (0)20 8731 8406
thespaniards
hampstead.co.uk

One of the oldest pubs in London, The Spaniards Inn has racked up its fair share of strange stories over the years. It's easy to see why – the pub, which sits on the northern boundary of Hampstead Heath, is full of low beams, creaking floorboards and atmospheric nooks. Built in 1585 as a tollgate, the coaching inn is said to have welcomed poets Byron, Shelley and Keats, as well as infamous highwayman Dick Turpin. If you're lucky (or unlucky, depending on your feelings about unexplained apparitions), you might spy a wandering woman in white or the spirit of Turpin stalking the street outside.

303 THE GRENADIER

18 Wilton Row
SW1X 7NR
Belgravia ⑤
+44 (0)20 7235 3074
grenadier
belgravia.com

Visitors traditionally hang money from the ceiling in this tiny former officers' mess. Why? Legend has it that Cedric, a young soldier, was caught cheating at cards and beaten to death. Now pub-goers do their bit to pay his debt, but ghostly goings-on continue, with pub staff and guests continuing to report spooky sighs and footsteps.

304 THE FLASK

77 Highgate West
Hill
N6 6BU
North ⑭
+44 (0)20 8348 7346
theflaskhighgate.com

This historic Highgate pub is a popular spot for walkers to refuel after a ramble on the Heath. The characterful building dates back to the early 18th century, though the stable block was built in the 1660s. Alfresco tables in the courtyard are popular all year round, while inside the pub's original features create an intriguing atmosphere. Here for the poltergeists? Look out for the ghost of a Spanish barmaid in the cellar and a man in a Cavalier uniform in the main bar – or head to the pub's committee room, which was supposedly the setting for one of the first ever autopsies using a body stolen from nearby Highgate Cemetery. It's enough to give you chills.

Old
COMMUNITY CLUBS

305 EFFRA SOCIAL
89 Effra Road
SW2 1DF
South ⑬
+44 (0)20 7737 6800
effrasocial.com

A Conservative Party club from the 19th century until 2012, Effra Social is now a buzzy bar, restaurant and events space with a dance hall, old-fashioned stage and plenty of tatty original features. Faded memorabilia from the building's political past line the walls, while you can travel back to the 1970s in the Churchill Room, a restored space with original furniture and a huge retro fireplace. Why the Churchill Room? Rumour has it the former Prime Minister drank here from time to time with his Tory pals.

306 BETHNAL GREEN WORKING MEN'S CLUB
42-46 Pollard Row
E2 6NB
East ⑪
+44 (0)20 7739 7170
workersplaytime.net

You can go to a 2000s disco, a *RuPaul's Drag Race* viewing party or a cabaret-inspired club night at Bethnal Green Working Men's Club these days. Dating back to 1887, the space was at one time a real East End working men's club, but it's far from traditional now. Visit this friendly and diverse club and you'll find a shrine to kitsch, quirk and sticky carpets.

307 MOTH CLUB
AT: OLD TRADES HALL
Valette St
E9 6NU
Hackney ⑩
+44 (0)20 8985 7963
mothclub.co.uk

A former members' club for military veterans, Moth (which stands for Memorable Order of Tin Hats) Club was revamped and opened as a new yet gloriously retro nightlife venue in 2015. Many of the building's original features are intact – the vintage checkerboard flooring, beautiful old dancefloor, signage and dark wooden bar area – but it's been jazzed up with modern touches, like the gold glittery ceiling.

Victorian
GIN PALACES

308 THE VIADUCT TAVERN

126 Newgate St
EC1A 7AA
City of London ②
+44 (0)20 7600 1863
viaducttavern.co.uk

The late Victorian decor inside this pub is enough to distract you from your drink. Look around to spot etched glass panels, tall mirrors and paintings of Pre-Raphaelite-style figures, all topped with a rich, red decorative ceiling. The pub first opened as a Victorian gin palace in 1869 and is staying true to form with a lengthy gin list and a menu of convict-themed G&T serves, inspired by the pub's proximity to the Central Criminal Court.

309 THE QUEENS

26 Broadway Parade
N8 9DE
North ⑭
+44 (0)20 8340 2031
foodandfuel.co.uk/the-queens-crouch-end

Built around the turn of the 20th century, this grand pub is still proudly intact, complete with art nouveau stained-glass windows and a mosaic floor at the entrance. The space is split up by decorative partitions – a throwback to the Victorians who liked privacy while they drank – with a huge original bar at its heart. These days the punters are a lot more sociable. You'll find groups playing board games, eating sharing platters crowded around tables or in the pub's pretty beer garden.

310 THE SALISBURY

90 St Martin's Lane
WC2N 4AP
Covent Garden ①
+44 (0)20 7836 5863
greeneking-pubs.co.uk

Busy with theatregoers and local workers, this enormous pub in Covent Garden gleams with pretty etched glass panels. The richly decorated 'turn of the century' interiors and sweeping mahogany bar date from around 1900. Look out for the original candelabras, made to look like women holding glowing flowers.

311 PRINCESS LOUISE

208 High Holborn
WC1V 7EP
Holborn ①
+44 (0)20 7405 8816
princesslouisepub.co.uk

You can't help but be impressed by the original tiles, mirrors and intricate mosaics that adorn the inside of this Holborn pub. The interiors have survived since the 1890s, along with a real sense of the building's Victorian past. Don't leave without taking a peek at the men's toilets – even the marble urinal in this pub is Grade II-listed.

308 **THE VIADUCT TAVERN**

Bars in
UNUSUAL SETTINGS

312 **WC**
Clapham Common
South Side
SW4 7AA
South ⑫
+44 (0)20 7622 5502
wcclapham.co.uk

An Edwardian public toilet might not sound like a great place for a bar, but somehow it's actually pretty charming. WC (which in this instance also stands for wine and charcuterie) is underground in a former water closet, where loads of the toilet's features have been retained – and disinfected, obviously. Original tiles line the walls and floor, skylights stud the ceiling and cubicle doors have been turned into tables.

313 **TOOTING TRAM AND SOCIAL**
46-48 Mitcham Road
SW17 9NA
South ⑫
+44 (0)20 8767 0278
tootingtram andsocial.co.uk

Once a store for the horse-drawn trams that moved Londoners around the city before buses and underground trains did, this Victorian tram shed has been converted into a bar, club and live music venue. Cosy sofas and vintage knick-knacks are crammed into corners and along a mezzanine, while the double-height centre of the hall makes the perfect dance floor. Check out the original Victorian glass tiles on the walls.

314 **THE SHIP AND SHOVELL**
1-3 Craven Passage
WC2N 5PH
Covent Garden ①
+44 (0)20 7839 1311
shipandshovell.co.uk

You have to pick a side when you visit this old-fashioned London boozer. One of the quirkiest watering holes in the capital, The Ship and Shovell is split into two halves by an alleyway. Punters can order drinks from either side of the street, while the 18th-century pubs, with their matching red façades, are linked by a tunnel which contains the kitchen and cellar.

315 **THE OLD BANK OF ENGLAND**

194 Fleet St
EC4A 2LT
Holborn ①
+44 (0)20 7430 2255
oldbankofengland.com

You'll struggle to keep your eyes on your pint at The Old Bank of England, an ornately decorated pub set in a former branch of The Bank of England. It operated as a bank from 1888 to 1975 and is now a stunning, and sizeable, public house with a gilded ceiling, decorative pillars and huge windows. Sit on the mezzanine level to survey your surroundings. Interestingly, this pub stands a few metres away from where the barbershop belonging to Sweeney Todd, the so-called 'demon barber of Fleet Street', once stood.

316 **THE OLD DAIRY**

1-3 Crouch Hill
N4 4AP
North ⑭
+44 (0)20 7263 3337
theolddairyn4.co.uk

This chilled pub calls the former Friern Manor Dairy Farm, established in 1836, home. Inside it's all exposed brickwork and high ceilings, with nods to the building's farming history, but the outside of the pub is the real draw. The decorative frontage features sgraffito murals that depict the dairy processes, such as grazing, milking, cooling and old-style delivery. Visiting on a Tuesday? Once you've admired the friezes, stay for the pub's 'Not Just An Udder Quiz'.

316 **THE OLD DAIRY**

CENTURIES-OLD
public houses

———————

317 THE DOVE

19 Upper Mall
W6 9TA
West ⑭
+44 (0)20 8748 9474
dovehammersmith.co.uk

Pubs don't get much more inviting than The Dove. The petite Thames-side spot is picture-book pretty, with cosy, wonky interiors (a tiny space at the front of the pub is officially the smallest barroom in the world) and a terrace with tables perched right on the riverside. The 18th-century boozer, which has been owned by local brewery Fuller's since 1796, is said to have been a favourite with King Charles II, who allegedly met his mistress Nell Gwynne here. It's easy to see why the historic spot could have been a royal fave.

318 THE LAMB & FLAG

33 Rose St
WC2E 9EB
Covent Garden ①
+44 (0)20 7497 9504
*lambandflagcovent
garden.co.uk*

A pub was first recorded on this site in 1772, and these days it's rare to see this much-loved Covent Garden watering hole without a cluster of drinkers spilling out on to the pavement at the front. Much of the pub was rebuilt in the 1950s, but parts still date back to the 18th century. It's popular with an after-work crowd, but if you'd visited in the early 19th century it would have been a different scene altogether – the pub was nicknamed 'The Bucket of Blood' thanks to its reputation for bare-knuckle prizefighting.

319 THE HOLLY BUSH

22 Holly Mount
NW3 6SG
North (14)
+44 (0)20 7435 2892
hollybush
hampstead.co.uk

If you need somewhere to warm your toes after a stomp on Hampstead Heath there's really only one place to go. Built in 1797 as stables for a nearby grand house, The Holly Bush opened as a quaint, low-ceilinged pub in the early 20th century. On a chilly day, spots by the open fires are in high demand.

320 THE FRENCH HOUSE

49 Dean St
W1D 5BG
Soho (1)
+44 (0)20 7437 2477
frenchhousesoho.com

The French House is an iconic Soho drinking den where you can expect no music, no phones, no laptops and no pints (beer, famously, is only served in halves here). Opened in the 1890s, The French House has welcomed the likes of Charles de Gaulle and Dylan Thomas over the years. Visit to have a delicious, long lunch in the upstairs bar or sip a half and people-watch on the pavement outside.

321 THE COACH & HORSES SOHO

29 Greek St
W1D 5DH
Soho (1)
+44 (0)20 7437 5920
coachandhorses
soho.pub

This colourful Soho establishment has been entertaining punters for hundreds of years. The protected corner pub, once well known for having one of the rudest landlords in London, could never be accused of being bland. Artists Francis Bacon and Lucian Freud, actors Peter O'Toole and John Hurt, and a host of *Private Eye* writers are known to have frequented the bar, while these days it's the setting for regular, rowdy sing-a-longs around the piano. The current building was constructed in 1847, though it's the pub's incredible, intact 1930s interiors that make it a nostalgic landmark. Step inside and you'll find original signage, light oak panelling and a little-altered layout, giving a tangible sense of how the pub would have felt almost a century ago.

Pubs with
INCREDIBLE INTERIORS

322 **THE PRINCE ALFRED**

5-A Formosa St
W9 1EE
West ⑬
+44 (0)20 7286 3287
theprincealfred.com

Welcoming punters since 1856, The Prince Alfred is a stellar example of how the Victorians liked their pubs. Inside you'll find pristine glass and timber 'snob screens', which split the bar up into separate areas for different social groups, all with their own external entrances. Check out the colourful original tiling and mosaic floor – or head down into the basement to find intimate tables in a space originally used for storing coal.

323 **THE WARRINGTON HOTEL**

93 Warrington Crescent
W9 1EH
West ⑬
+44 (0)20 7286 8282
thewarrington.co.uk

Stunning tiled columns and a mosaic floor welcome you to this opulent Victorian boozer. First built in 1858, this pub with five rooms is elaborately decorated, with stained-glass windows, art nouveau friezes and a beautiful marble-topped bar. Go to gawp at it in all its glory, and stay for the elegantly done, classic pub grub.

324 **CROCKER'S FOLLY**

24 Aberdeen Place
NW8 8JR
West ⑬
+44 (0)20 7289 9898
crockersfolly.com

This grand pub is astonishingly pretty. A recent restoration has brought the building's late-Victorian features back to life. The saloon bar features around 50 types of marble, with ornamental pillars and delicate plasterwork ceilings, while original chandeliers twinkle throughout. If you can keep your eyes off your surroundings long enough to peruse the menu, you'll find classic cocktails and Lebanese food.

325 THE BLACKFRIAR

174 Queen Victoria St
EC4V 4EG
City of London ②
+44 (0)20 7236 5474
nicholsonspubs.co.uk/
theblackfriarblack
friarslondon

There's something surreal about this slim, wedge-shaped pub, standing solo near Blackfriars station. It's a beacon of art nouveau style, built in the 1870s on the site of a Dominican friary (hence the name) and remodelled in 1905 by arts and crafts sculptors Frederick T. Callcott and Henry Poole, who we have to thank for the pub's unique and lavish interiors. Spot jolly-looking friars dotted around the place, alongside great swathes of marble, glittering mosaics and witty friezes, depicting the life of monks and titled with phrases like 'Don't advertise, tell a gossip' and 'Contentment surpasses riches'.

326 CITTIE OF YORKE

22 High Holborn
WC1V 6BN
Holborn ①
+44 (0)20 7242 7670

Expect bargain beer and bags of character in this mock-medieval pub. Stepping inside is like walking onto the set of a period drama, and for good reason. Though made to look like the kind of pub Shakespeare would have drank in, the Cittie of Yorke was actually built in the 1920s. Head straight to the rear bar, which masquerades as a Tudor hall with a cavernous roof, enormous wooden vats and seats in sought-after ornately carved booths.

327 THE CHURCHILL ARMS

119 Kensington
Church St
W8 7LN
Kensington ④
+44 (0)20 7727 4242
churchillarms
kensington.co.uk

No surprise that The Churchill Arms is big on patriotism. Renamed in honour of the former Prime Minister after WWII (its only connection being that Winston Churchill's grandparents used to drink here), the cosy pub is stuffed to the rafters with wartime memorabilia – first aid boxes, lamps, pots, medals, models and tankards hang from the ceiling. But, really, it's the Victorian pub's exterior that draws the crowds. Draped in blooming greenery during the summer months and swamped by nearly 100 glowing Christmas trees in the winter, this quirky pub is always a looker.

20TH-CENTURY
drinking dens

328 THE ELEPHANT AND CASTLE

119 Newington
Causeway
SE1 6BN
South ⑫
+44 (0)20 7403 8124
*elephantandcastle
pub.com*

The Elephant and Castle pub was first recorded on this site in 1765 and, incredibly, the entire area was named after it in the 18th century. But the place you'll find there today, which was also a hub of UK garage music in the 1990s, is pure 1960s. The building, in the basement of Metro Central Heights, a glass and metal high-rise designed by Ernö Goldfinger as offices for the Ministry of Health, dates from 1966 – check out the pebble-dashed frontage and waffle ceiling.

329 THE IVY HOUSE

40 Stuart Road
SE15 3BE
South ⑫
+44 (0)20 7277 8233
ivyhousenunhead.com

This community favourite is London's first co-operatively owned pub. After it was closed down in 2012, locals raised money to buy the freehold and The Ivy House now has 371 shareholders. Built in the 1930s on the site of a late-19th-century pub, the Grade II-listed spot is a gloriously well-preserved example of an interwar 'improved public house', a new breed of pub designed to boost visitor numbers. Just look at the incredible music hall-style stage, where you can now catch live music, film screenings and spoken word.

330 THE DUKE

7 Roger St
WC1N 2PB
Bloomsbury ⑦
+44 (0)20 7242 7230
dukepub.co.uk

Built in the late 1930s, this Bloomsbury boozer was sporting stylish pink walls well before millennials claimed the colour. The Grade II-listed pub's interiors are surprisingly intact. Think period panelling, art deco mirrors, original booths and a wooden bar that's been propping up visitors for 80 years. Pop by for a tipple and a traditional homemade pie, with a side order of nostalgia.

331 PALM TREE

127 Grove Road
E3 5BH
East ⑪
+44 (0)20 8980 2918

This unique pub, standing alone in greenery beside Regent's Canal, was once in a built up part of the East End. The only building on its street to survive extensive bombing during the Blitz, it's now something of a relic. It was built in 1935 on the site of a 19th-century public house, and the 1930s vibe is still evident today, with original interiors – gold wallpaper, heavy curtains, jazzy carpets – and a bar where you can only pay with cash.

332 THE PHOENIX ARTS CLUB

1 Phoenix St
WC2H 8BU
Covent Garden ①
+44 (0)20 7836 1077
phoenixartsclub.com

Head down a set of steps from street level to find this theatrical bar, restaurant and club beneath the West End's streets. The late-night spot, which opened as a bar in 1988, is located in the original dressing and rehearsal rooms of The Phoenix Theatre and stays true to its roots: walls are plastered with signed headshots, posters and memorabilia from past screen and stage productions. Keep your eyes peeled for famous faces who have been known to take part in the weekly musical theatre open mic nights. Phoenix Arts Club is a members' club, but non-members are welcome if they book ahead. Just seen a play? Flashing your ticket on the door will get you entry too.

333 THE CARPENTERS ARMS

73 Cheshire St
E2 6EG
East ⑪
+44 (0)20 7739 6342
carpentersarms
freehouse.com

You wouldn't know it today but this bright pub serving small plates and Sunday roasts was once the most notorious drinking den in the city. Bought by East End gangster twins Reggie and Ronnie Kray in 1967, The Carpenters Arms was supposedly a present for their mother Violet. The brothers grew up in a house close by at 178 Vallance Road.

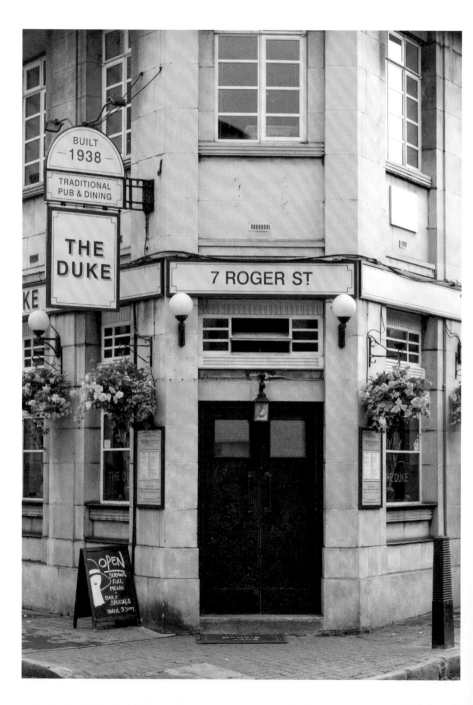

HAZLITT'S

STAYS

London's
OLDEST *hotels*

---

334 BROWN'S HOTEL

Albemarle St
W1S 4BP
Mayfair ⑥
+44 (0)20 7493 6020
*roccofortehotels.com/
browns-hotel*

Luxurious Brown's Hotel might just be London's oldest hotel. It opened in 1837 – the same year that Queen Victoria took to the throne – and has attracted impressive clientele over the years, from royalty and foreign dignitaries to Theodore Roosevelt, Rudyard Kipling, Orson Welles and Alexander Graham Bell. Despite renovations, the ultra-traditional, elegant essence of Brown's Hotel is intact. Just stepping into the English Tea Room – a wood panelled space where Queen Vic reportedly enjoyed afternoon tea – is proof of that.

335 GREAT NORTHERN HOTEL

Pancras Road
N1C 4TB
King's Cross ⑦
+44 (0)20 3388 0800
gnhlondon.com

One of the first purpose-built railway hotels in the country, the Great Northern Hotel opened in 1854 to serve passengers at the start or end of their journeys. Designed by Lewis Cubitt, the bold building captured the glamour of the age of steam trains. These days, the hotel looks out over King's Cross station's modern concourse, which was designed to follow the curved edge of the hotel. It's surrounded by commuters, suitcase-wielding travellers and the sound of modern train announcements, but inside you'd never know.

336 THE SAVOY

Strand
WC2R 0EZ
Covent Garden ①
+44 (0)20 7836 4343
fairmont.com/
savoy-london

The world-famous Savoy hotel first opened its doors in 1889. It's as luxe and high glamour now as it was then, when it was considered cutting-edge with its electric lights and hydraulic lifts. The hotel has always been popular with the royal family, actors, artists and celebrities – famous faces like Marilyn Monroe, Marlene Dietrich and Bob Dylan (to name a few) have snoozed here. Follow in their footsteps and take in The Savoy's stunning interiors – each of the bedrooms pay tribute to the hotel's fashionable past, with dreamy Edwardian and art deco designs.

337 ST PANCRAS RENAISSANCE HOTEL

Euston Road
NW1 2AR
King's Cross ⑦
+44 (0)20 7841 3540
stpancraslondon.com

If you've ever wanted to recreate the iconic music video to Spice Girls' song *Wannabe*, you're in luck. The 1990s pop hit was recorded on this hotel's sweeping grand staircase. It was also used in filming for *Harry Potter and the Chamber of Secrets*, but there's history here going back much further than that. This turreted, castle-like hotel, which doubles up as the Gothic frontage for St Pancras International Station, first opened as the Midland Grand in 1873. After closing in 1935, the romantic Victorian building fell into ruin but was thankfully revived in the early 2010s as the St Pancras Renaissance Hotel, when many of the original details were restored. Stepping inside this extravagant, ornate hotel now feels as impressive as it would have done in the 1870s.

338 CLARIDGE'S

Brook St
W1K 4HR
Mayfair ⑥
+44 (0)20 7629 8860
claridges.co.uk

The epitome of art deco glamour, much of Claridge's, which first opened in 1856, hasn't been touched since it was decorated in the late 1920s. It's no time capsule but each modern addition or renovation is inspired by and sensitive to its jazz age past. Once you pass through the 100-year-old retro entrance, flanked by porters in top hats, you'll be greeted by gleaming interiors, original mirrors and delicate glass panels. The bedrooms are the perfect homage to the 1920s and 1930s, with polished glass, geometric designs and motifs from the hotel's history.

LONG-STANDING
hotels

339 THE RITZ LONDON

150 Piccadilly
W1J 9BR
Piccadilly ⑤
+44 (0)20 7493 8181
theritzlondon.com

The ultimate luxury destination since 1906, The Ritz was the
first hotel to be awarded a royal warrant for 'banqueting and
catering services'. It's also where the Queen chose to celebrate
her 80th birthday. Fancy, eh? The grand hotel, with its green
slate roof, has a Parisian feel to it and inside it's decked out
in sumptuous Louis XV style. Stay the night here and you'll
feel like you've woken up in another time – where gilded
fireplaces, marble bathtubs and personal butlers are the norm.
Fun fact: the Trafalgar Suite, which is decorated in celebration
of the Battle of Trafalgar in 1805, was where Hugh Grant and
Julia Roberts filmed scenes for the movie *Notting Hill*.

340 THE LANDMARK

222 Marylebone
Road
NW1 6JQ
Marylebone ⑥
+44 (0)20 7631 8000
landmarklondon.co.uk

There's nothing like a few indoor palm trees to make you
feel like you've wandered into another era. Built in 1899,
around the same time as neighbouring Marylebone station,
The Landmark is a huge heritage hotel built in red brick
around an enormous glass-roofed courtyard. Back then, guests
could make a grand entrance by horse and carriage directly
into the courtyard, while today the elegant space is a winter
garden where you can have light meals, brunch or traditional
afternoon tea beneath the palms. You can also peer out onto
the airy atrium from windows in the hotel's plush bedrooms.

341 THE GORING

15 Beeston Place
SW1W 0JW
Westminster ⑤
+44 (0)20 7396 9000
thegoring.com

This regal, five-star Edwardian hotel has been run by the same family since it opened in 1910. It's intimate, exclusive and unashamedly old-school. No surprise, then, that it's another favourite with the royals – Kate Middleton famously stayed here the night before her Westminster Abbey wedding, while it's held a royal warrant from the Queen since 2013. Look out for glimpses of Gainsborough silk wallpaper. The same silk lines walls in Buckingham Palace and was chosen to decorate first class sections of the ill-fated *RMS Titanic*.

342 THE CONNAUGHT

Carlos Place
W1K 2AL
Mayfair ⑥
+44 (0)20 7499 7070
the-connaught.co.uk

Christened The Connaught (after Queen Victoria's son Arthur, Duke of Connaught and Strathearn) in 1917, this Mayfair hotel is an elegant blend of past and present fashions where modern flourishes sit easily alongside historic details, original artworks and more classical design. For a taste of time gone by, book a Grosvenor Suite for 18th-century interiors, 24-hour butler service and a vintage cocktail cabinet.

343 MANDARIN ORIENTAL HYDE PARK

66 Knightsbridge
SW1X 7LA
Belgravia ⑤
+44 (0)20 7235 2000
mandarinoriental.com/
london

Queen Elizabeth and her sister Margaret are known to have taken dance lessons in the then-named Hyde Park Hotel's ballroom, while Winston Churchill holed up here on a number of occasions – once to form the SAS War Crime Investigating Team from a suite in the late 1940s. These days the luxe hotel is plush and richly decorated. Look out for original marble and mosaics, as well as sweeping views of Hyde Park from a number of the rooms.

Places for a **NOSTALGIC**
night's sleep

344 **HAZLITT'S**

6 Frith St
W1D 3JA
Soho ①
+44 (0)20 7434 1771
hazlittshotel.com

Staying over at Hazlitt's, an atmospheric hotel in a 300-year-old Soho townhouse, is like sleeping in a museum. Every room is evocatively decorated in rich hues, with creaky floorboards, vintage fittings and hefty four-poster beds. You'll be glad they've installed state-of-the-art bathrooms, though – the Georgians wouldn't have had running water, let alone rainforest showers. The hotel is named after essayist William Hazlitt, who died here in 1830 and, as the story goes, was then laid out under the bed by his landlady who was keen to re-let his rooms. You just try to go to sleep without checking under the bed first.

345 **ZETTER TOWNHOUSE**

49-50 St John's Sq
EC1V 4JJ
Clerkenwell ⑧
+44 (0)20 7324 4444
thezettertownhouse.
com/clerkenwell

Quirky and eclectic objects fill this 13-bedroom Georgian townhouse, which opened as a hotel in 2011. It's designed to feel like the home of an eccentric elderly aunt, and there's definitely something old school about the place. Check out the bold fabrics, antiques and pre-loved furniture plus nods to traditional British styling. Where else can you kip in a four-poster covered in Union Jack bunting?

346 **THE BEAUMONT**

8 Balderton St
W1K 6TF
Mayfair ⑥
+44 (0)20 7499 1001
thebeaumont.com

It's been open for less than a decade, but The Beaumont feels straight out of the 1920s. The hotel resides in a neoclassical style former car garage on Brown Hart Gardens. It was originally built in the late 1920s as luxury parking for shoppers heading to nearby Selfridges. The hotel's aesthetic is firmly rooted in the building's past. It's filled with original art, antiques and of-the-time interior style.

347 THE NED

27 Poultry
EC2R 8AJ
City of London ②
+44 (0)20 3828 2000
thened.com

A former disused bank, since 2017 this imposing building right in the middle of the City has been a glorious hotel and Soho House-run members' club that manages to both evoke days gone by and feel totally modern. Stay upstairs in the warren of swanky, 1920s-style rooms or simply visit the cavernous ground-floor space, which is home to eight restaurants, bars and atmospheric live music. The architecture of the building, designed by Sir Edwin 'Ned' Lutyens in 1924, dominates and there are countless original features still intact, like the imposing verdite columns and wrought-iron domed windows that line the banking hall. Venture down into the basement where you'll find The Vault, an extraordinary cocktail bar, open to members and hotel guests. Access is through the original bank vault door and the walls of the low-lit bar glint with thousands of security deposit boxes.

348 L'OSCAR LONDON

2-6 Southampton Row
WC1B 4AA
Holborn ⑩
+44 (0)20 7405 5555
loscar.com

Don't be tricked by L'oscar's unassuming exterior or the words 'The Baptist Church House', which are engraved onto the front of the building. Inside, the former Baptist church, built around the turn of the 20th century, is entirely transformed. Though plenty of the building's Grade II-listed, period features remain – the hotel restaurant is set in the octagonal, double-height chapel – the vibe inside is more lavish extravagance than pious prayer.

COOL PLACES
to stay

---

349 CLINK78

78 King's Cross Road
WC1X 9QG
Clerkenwell ⑧
+44 (0)20 7183 9400
clinkhostels.com/
clink78

Fancy spending a night snoozing inside a former prison cell? Formerly Clerkenwell Magistrates Court, this Victorian building is now a backpackers' hostel. Beds are available in the old cells, complete with original bunks, high windows and a heavy metal door (relax – you can open it from the inside). You can also hang out in the former courtroom or party in the basement bar, named ClashBar after the punk band that once went on trial here.

350 PRINCELET STREET

13 Princelet St
E1 6QH
Spitalfields ⑨
+44 (0)16 2882 5925
landmarktrust.org.uk

Bed down for the night on one of Spitalfields' most well-preserved historic streets. Like nearby Fournier Street, Princelet Street sprung up in the early 1700s and was populated with Huguenot silk weavers. This tall, elegant and carefully restored home is now owned by the Landmark Trust. Rent its four floors and peaceful walled garden for a taste of what life would have been like here centuries ago.

351 THE GEORGIAN HOUSE

AT: HAMPTON COURT
PALACE
KT8 9AU
East Molesey
+44 (0)16 2882 5925
landmarktrust.org.uk

Stay inside Hampton Court Palace's grounds at The Georgian House and you'll have free rein to wander through the gardens and courtyards after the rest of the visitors have gone home. The elegant house was actually built as a great kitchen while George I was on the throne in 1719. It later became two houses, for the Clerk of Works and the Gardener, and you can now rent one of them to live out any daydreams you have about royal court life.

INDEX

COLOPHON

EDITING *and* COMPOSING — Ellie Walker-Arnott

PHOTOGRAPHY — Sam Mellish — www.sammellish.com

GRAPHIC DESIGN — Joke Gossé and Sarah Schrauwen

COVER IMAGE — The Royal Arcade (#231)

The addresses in this book have been selected after thorough independent
research by the author, in collaboration with Luster Publishing. The selection
is solely based on personal evaluation of the business by the author. Nothing
in this book was published in exchange for payment or benefits of any kind.

D/2020/12.005/3

ISBN 978 94 6058 2677

NUR 450, 510

© 2020 Luster, Antwerp

www.lusterweb.com — WWW.THE500HIDDENSECRETS.COM

info@lusterweb.com

Printed in Italy by Printer Trento.